D1281850

KORN/FERRY INTERNATIONAL

powered by LOMINGER

DRIVER

FYI

For Talent Engagement™

Drivers of Best Practice

FOR MANAGERS AND BUSINESS LEADERS

Kim E. Ruyle, Robert W. Eichinger & Kenneth P. De Meuse

Table of Contents

Introduction

FYI for Talent Engagement™

Why We Wrote This Book

FYI for Talent Engagement™ is a companion to the Talent Engagement Architect™, a service offering designed to help organizations assess and increase levels of engagement in the general employee population *and* in targeted groups of high-potential employees. The focus on high-potential talent sets this solution apart from other general employee engagement surveys on the market.

While there are many surveys available that provide varying levels of diagnostic help for organizations, there are few resources available that provide targeted prescriptive guidance for improving engagement. That's what this book does. For each of the 11 research-based drivers of engagement, we've provided 10 development tips—specific actions that organizations can take to move the needle on engagement. To enable deeper understanding of each driver, we've also provided a list of related resources and suggested readings.

As we work with organizations to help them develop leaders who are more skilled in engaging employees, we have many resources at our disposal that complement the content in this book. We've mapped each of the Engagement Driver items to the competencies in the Lominger Leadership Architect® Competency Library. In addition, we've mapped Engagement Driver items to Organizational Capabilities and identified complementary remedies from Lominger's Strategic Effectiveness Architect™. This mapping is invaluable when developing comprehensive action plans that increase engagement and provide sustainability by developing key organizational capabilities.

Senior executives, line managers, and talent management practitioners will find this book useful for enhancing change initiatives, leadership development, and organizational effectiveness. Numerous studies and surveys show that measurement without action not only doesn't help, it can actually decrease engagement. So if you choose to measure engagement, you should also commit to act on the results. This book will help you get there.

The Structure of This Book

After a broad-based view of employee engagement in the first chapter, we specifically focus on the engagement of high-potential talent in the second chapter. The remaining 11 book chapters are devoted to the Engagement Drivers. The drivers represent key factors in organizations that directly impact levels of employee engagement. These are the primary causes of engagement and, for the most part, are within an organization's control. These drivers, then, should be the focus of efforts to enhance engagement.

Driver A: Strategic Alignment

Driver B: Trust in Senior Leadership

Driver C: Immediate Manager Working Relationship

Driver D: Peer Culture

Driver E: Personal Influence

Driver F: Nature of My Career

Driver G: Career Support

Driver H: Nature of the Job

Driver I: Developmental Opportunities

Driver J: Employee Recognition

Driver K: Pay Fairness

Each of the 11 chapters addresses a different Engagement Driver and includes the following sections:

- **Quotes** – To stimulate thinking about the particular Engagement Driver.
- **The Signpost** – A brief description of the Engagement Driver and its importance.
- **Unskilled** – A list of descriptors that apply to organizations that do not demonstrate strength in that particular Engagement Driver.
- **Skilled** – A list of descriptors that apply to organizations that demonstrate exceptional strength in that particular Engagement Driver.
- **Some Causes** – A list of some of the root causes that can explain why an organization is weak in the Engagement Driver.
- **The Ten Leadership Architect® Competencies Most Associated with This Driver (in order of connectedness)** – A listing of the ten most strongly related individual competencies from the Leadership Architect® that support success in the Engagement Driver.
  - As indicated in the heading, the ordering of the ten competencies is based on the strength of the relationship between the competency and the Engagement Driver—those higher in the list have a stronger relationship.
  - Use the competency lists to understand what particular skills, experience, and knowledge leaders need to support that Engagement Driver.
  - Also, use these competencies in interviewing, selecting, assessing, developing, and deploying managers.
- **The Map** – A description of the Engagement Driver to provide a broad context. The map explains key elements of the driver, their importance, and how successful organizations leverage those elements to create an engaging workplace.

- **Some Remedies** – Suggestions for actions organizations can take to enhance effectiveness in the Engagement Driver.
  - These prescriptive recommendations are similar to what you might find in an individual's development plan but are directed to the organizational level.
- **Suggested Readings** – A reference list of resources we've found useful in learning about and further exploring issues related to each Engagement Driver.
  - We've explored both the theoretical and the practical, with a bias toward accessible references that will serve as springboards to your understanding of best practices and applications.

Each chapter covering an Engagement Driver stands on its own with the information provided to answer the basic question: What does it take to do this as well as it can be done?

What Can the Talent Engagement Architect™ Do for Your Organization?

Your employees enter the job on their first day with a set of attitudes that influence their behavior. Over time, the work environment created by your leadership will affect their attitudes, for better or for worse. And since behavior typically follows on the heels of attitude, the work environment you create will also have a significant impact on employee behaviors, on their performance.

The Talent Engagement Architect™ is a full-service offering that includes resources (such as this book), instruments (such as the Talent Engagement Architect™ Survey), and consulting and training support that can help you create the work environment that attracts, engages, and retains top talent.

Organizations can use the Talent Engagement Architect™ to:

- Assess engagement levels in the general employee population.
- Assess engagement levels in employee sub-populations, including high-potential employees.
- Diagnose root causes of engagement problems.
- Identify and prioritize actions to drive engagement.
- Develop the competencies in managers that will make them effective at engagement.

The war for talent is real, and the organizations winning that war are the ones proactively creating work environments that engage their top talent.

Kim E. Ruyle

Robert W. Eichinger

Kenneth P. De Meuse

About the Authors

Kim Ruyle

Kim Ruyle is vice president of product development for Lominger International. He started his career in the skilled trades, taught at several universities, founded and managed a software company, and held management positions in Fortune 500 and Global 100 organizations. Kim has presented at over 50 national and international conferences in the human resource and learning and development fields, authored many articles and book chapters, and served on editorial boards and numerous expert panels. He is also certified as a Senior Professional in Human Resources (SPHR) from the Society for Human Resource Management and is a recipient of numerous awards in the industry. Kim coauthored *FYI for Strategic Effectiveness*™ with Bob Eichinger and Dave Ulrich, and *FYI for Performance Management*™ with Bob Eichinger and Mike Lombardo.

Bob Eichinger

Bob Eichinger is vice chairman of the Korn/Ferry Institute for Korn/Ferry International. Prior to Korn/Ferry's acquisition of Lominger International, he was cofounder and CEO of Lominger Limited, Inc. and cocreator of the Leadership Architect® Suite of management, executive, and organizational development tools. During his 40+ year career, he has worked inside companies such as PepsiCo and Pillsbury, and as a consultant in Fortune 500 companies in the United States, Europe, Japan, Canada, and Australia. Dr. Eichinger lectures extensively on the topic of executive and management development and has served on the Board of the Human Resource Planning Society. He has worked as a coach with more than 1,000 managers and executives. Some of his books include *The Leadership Machine*, written with Mike Lombardo, *100 Things You Need to Know: Best People Practices for Managers & HR*, written with Mike Lombardo and Dave Ulrich, and *FYI for Strategic Effectiveness*™, written with Kim Ruyle and Dave Ulrich.

Ken De Meuse

Ken De Meuse is associate vice president of research at Lominger International. Prior to joining Lominger, he was on the faculties at the University of Wisconsin – Eau Claire, Iowa State University, and the University of Nebraska at Omaha. Ken has published numerous articles on employee attitudes and organizational behavior in several leading journals. He has appeared on ABC News, CNN, AP Radio, and National Public Radio and has been featured in national publications such as the *Wall Street Journal*, *BusinessWeek*, *Fortune*, *U.S. News & World Report*, the *New York Times*, and *USA Today* for his expertise on the impact organizational change has on the workforce. More than 100 universities and 150 corporations have contacted him regarding his research work in this area. Ken coauthored *Resizing the Organization: Managing Layoffs, Divestitures, and Closings* with Mitchell Marks and also coauthored *50 More Things You Need to Know: The Science Behind Best People Practices for Managers & HR Professionals* with Dave Ulrich, Bob Eichinger, and John Kulas.

Acknowledgements

We are indebted to a number of people who contributed ideas and assistance in the preparation of this book.

Guangrong Dai did an outstanding job researching the drivers of engagement and the particular factors that impact high-potential engagement. He constructed and piloted many survey versions and put his skills in statistics and analysis to very good use.

King Yii (Lulu) Tang conducted a very thorough literature review and combed through hundreds of research studies, articles, and books to ensure we were current and had good sources to recommend.

George Hallenbeck and Vicki Swisher contributed significant content, served as sounding boards, and read and marked up every paragraph of every page with terrific suggestions to improve the book.

Lesley Kurke, Diane Hoffmann, and Zach Schaap did an excellent job of design, layout, and production.

Michelle Weitzman has significant experience in the area of employee engagement, was an important contributor to the design of the solution, and continues to be an engagement evangelist.

Dee Gaeddert, Craig Sneltjes, Paul Stiles, Kay Owen, Terry Enlow, Sarah Pettit, Susanne Ingerson, and Lisa-Marie Hanson made many helpful suggestions.

As a Lominger customer, Laurie Schamber collaborated extensively with Lominger on one of the early applications of the Talent Engagement Architect™. She was a pleasure to work with and helped shape our thinking around high-potential engagement.

Bonnie Parks, as always, did an outstanding job of proofreading and editing our manuscript.

We appreciate the contribution of all.

Chapter 1
Fundamentals of Employee Engagement

If you want to capture the economic high ground in the creative economy,
you need employees who are more than acquiescent, attentive and astute—
they must also be zestful, zany and zealous.
Gary Hamel – Management consultant, professor, and author

Will You Know It When You See It?

What makes a good employee? What do you look for when recruiting new talent to your organization? Managers generally identify three primary requirements. The *skill set* is surely important—the knowledge, skills, and abilities required for the job. For many roles above entry-level, *experience* is also important for the confidence, maturity, and perspective it provides. And rounding out the primary requirements: *attitude*.

Attitude—a big construct with lots of dimensions. Job-related attitudes can be difficult to assess and, because they're sensitive to workplace conditions, are subject to significant variation over time. So what attitudes do you look for in an employee? Do you value enthusiasm? Surely you do. Who doesn't value enthusiasm? But does enthusiasm trump loyalty? What about commitment? Respect? Obedience? Dedication? Satisfaction? What attitudes really count?

For nearly a century, management researchers have been investigating the link between attitudes and productivity. When Elton Mayo studied the link between working conditions and productivity in his famous series of experiments known as the Hawthorne Studies, the findings had a large, enduring impact on the study of employee motivation and job-related attitudes. Rensis Likert developed his well-known five-point Likert Scale in an effort to assess employee attitudes and find support for his thesis that a humanistic approach to supervision was more effective than a directive, task-based approach. Since those early studies, many researchers have examined various dimensions of employee attitudes— Morale, Job Satisfaction; Job Involvement; Employee Empowerment, etc. (See figure 1 for a historical perspective.)

So, after countless research studies conducted over many years, what have we learned about employee attitudes? How important is attitude to employee performance? Do satisfied employees outperform their less satisfied peers? Are happy workers more productive? If you improve workplace conditions or benefits to improve morale, can you be assured of increased output and higher quality?

1

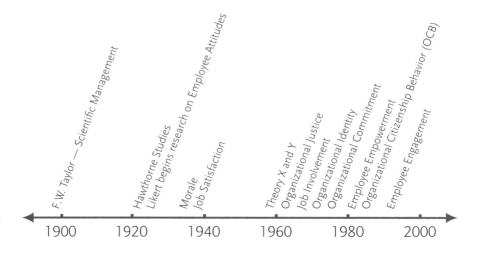

Fig. 1. Evolution of Employee Attitude Assessment

The short answer is no. There are no consistent research findings that correlate employee attitudes such as job satisfaction or morale to performance. Although you're more likely to retain satisfied workers than dissatisfied workers, you can't assume that the satisfied workers are the most productive.

Discouraging? Counterintuitive? Perhaps. But the research is clear. If you want to establish a link between employee attitude and job performance, you've got to come at it from a different angle—the engagement angle. Employee engagement is more than employee morale, job satisfaction, or employee involvement. Employee engagement is comprised of both attitude and behavior.

We model our definition and measure of engagement after Schaufeli and his colleagues (Salanova, González-Romá, & Bakker, 2002). They contend engagement entails three integrated factors—vigor, dedication, and absorption. Vigor relates to an employee possessing (a) a high level of energy and mental resilience while working, (b) being willing to personally invest effort into one's work, and (c) being persistent, even when faced with work difficulties. Dedication pertains to having a sense of significance, enthusiasm, inspiration, pride, and challenge in one's work. And finally, absorption consists of (a) fully concentrating and being deeply engrossed in one's job, (b) feeling the time passes quickly while working, and (c) having difficulty detaching oneself from work.

Very importantly, for engaged employees these attitudinal elements of engagement are aligned with the goals of the organization. Engaged employees

2

care about the right things—the things that best serve the organization. They feel a personal responsibility exhibited by:

- Caring about the future of the organization.
- Viewing the organization's problems as their own.
- Taking (or being ready to take) a stand on behalf of the organization.

The attitude of engaged employees drives them to do more, more than they must to simply keep their jobs. They expend discretionary effort exhibited by:

- Working harder and longer than is expected.
- Volunteering for additional assignments, projects, and weekend work.
- Performing a host of organizational citizen behaviors (OCBs).

Yes, if you look for the right indicators, you will know engagement when you see it. Engaged employees are more productive because their work behavior is energized, focused, and more aligned to the needs of the organization. Engaged employees are more likely to remain with the company because they are challenged by their work in the context of a supportive environment with a caring, encouraging, and empowering boss. They feel appreciated, listened to, and supported. They believe in the mission and vision of their organization and sense that the executive leadership of the organization can successfully lead it in the future.

These elements are summarized in our formal definition of employee engagement:

Employee engagement is a mind-set in which employees take personal stakeholder responsibility for the success of the organization and apply discretionary efforts aligned with its goals.

Why Should You Care?

Organizations with engaged employees outperform those organizations with less engaged employees. It's that simple. The link between employee engagement and organizational performance is powerful and well documented. Engagement is a business imperative, not just a nice thing to do. It is an important lever top management can use to achieve organizational goals. You can choose to pull the lever or not, at your own peril.

Many studies have found results supporting the financial benefits of employee engagement. For example:

- Sales teams who were more engaged outperformed lower-engaged teams by $2 million (Vance, 2006).
- Employee engagement at companies demonstrating double-digit growth exceeded engagement in slower-growth companies by 20% (Hewitt Associates, 2004).

3

- At a brewery, it was found that engaged employees were five times less likely than unengaged employees to be involved in a safety-related incident and seven times less likely to have a lost-time safety incident (Vance, 2006).

- The Corporate Leadership Council reported that highly engaged employees outperformed average employees by 20% (Corporate Leadership Council, 2004).

- The Corporate Leadership Council also reported that highly engaged employees were 87% less likely to leave their organizations (Corporate Leadership Council, 2004).

- Fleming, Coffman, and Harter (2005) found that departments with engaged employees had double the sales of departments with disengaged employees.

- Schneider (2006) found that engaged employees increased the organization's return on investment by an average of 11.4%.

- Harter, Schmidt, and Hayes (2002) observed that highly engaged business units outproduced less engaged ones across various jobs and industries. The most engaged units had roughly $100,000 more revenue per month on average.

Multiple studies in a variety of industries have shown that an increase in employee engagement results in improvements in profitability, quality, productivity, revenue, customer satisfaction, innovation, and retention. Likewise, other metrics decline: turnover, accidents, absenteeism, shrinkage due to employee theft, and employee grievances.

The potential value of engagement contrasted with the engagement levels in most firms represents a tremendous opportunity. Only about 25% of workers appear to be truly engaged in their jobs (Bates, 2004; Kabachnick, 2006). Due in part to this low level of engagement, Bates concluded that the U.S. economy is running at only 30% capacity. The employee engagement problem is not limited to the United States. A study conducted by The Conference Board found the level of engagement across five regions of the world (Asia, Eastern Europe, Western Europe, Latin America, and the United States) to be largely the same (Gibbons, 2006). In Britain, for example, it was found that fully 20% of workers were disengaged, at an estimated cost to the British economy of $64 billion to $66 billion per year (Flade, 2004). A 2002 Gallup poll reported that disengaged employees cost American organizations more than $250 billion a year (Kabachnick, 2006).

The importance of having highly engaged employees appears more important than ever today. Back in the 1950s and 1960s, there was a close and enduring relationship between employees and their companies. Employees tended to be loyal to their employer, often staying for their entire career. In return,

4

the company provided a safe, secure workplace for as long as the employee wanted. Such a long-term arrangement fostered workplace stability, collegiality, and stressed performing at an adequate level (De Meuse & Tornow, 1990). Scholars refer to this unwritten, implicit agreement between employers and employees as a "psychological contract" (see Rousseau, 1995).

Much has changed during the past two decades of globalization, mergers and acquisitions, and corporate restructurings and downsizings. This psychological contract has been modified. One study found that Harvard MBAs, on average, changed companies three to four times during their first ten years out of school (Reichheld, 2001). In this new era of boundaryless careers (Arthur & Rousseau, 1996), employees typically no longer pursue employment loyalty and stability. Rather, they search for companies that provide career growth, job challenge, professional development, work flexibility, and employability (e.g., Lockwood, 2007; Ulrich, Eichinger, Kulas, & De Meuse, 2007). In short, employees are looking for companies that will engage them. Employee engagement is a key predictor of an organization's ability to attract and retain talent, especially top talent.

Engagement Index

To use a medical analogy, the level of engagement in an organization is an important measure of its health. An engagement survey, using this analogy, can be thought of as a test to assess the health of a patient, in this case, the engagement health of an organization. The Talent Engagement Architect™ Survey was designed to measure both the presenting symptoms of engagement health as well as the root causes of those symptoms.

There are ten items in the survey to assess symptoms; we call this set of items the *Engagement Index*. The items assess three dimensions of engagement:

- Organizational Pride
- Work Dedication
- Retention

The focus of the index is to directly measure an employee's level of engagement in the company. The content for the ten items that assess these dimensions was derived from the theoretical and empirical research cited in the literature (Kahn, 1990; Konrad, 2006; Schaufeli et al., 2002; Wiley, 2007). These items comprise emotions, cognitions, and behavioral intentions.

Engagement Drivers

Employee engagement has been one of the most frequently examined concepts during the past decade. Numerous studies have been conducted to measure employee engagement (Schaufeli et al., 2002; Sonnentag, 2003; Wiley, 2007).

And numerous studies have attempted to identify what work-related factors cause engagement.

A Conference Board study identified 29 different causes of engagement measured by various researchers in the literature (Gibbons, 2006). The following eight were the most cited: (1) trust and integrity of management team, (2) nature of the job/work, (3) line-of-sight of impact of contributions on company performance, (4) career growth opportunities, (5) overall pride in the company, (6) relationship with coworkers/team, (7) employee development opportunities, and (8) relationship with immediate manager. Other research has found three additional factors to be important to engagement—employee recognition, pay fairness, and the amount of personal influence an employee possesses (Robinson, Perryman, & Hayday, 2004; Swindall, 2007; Towers Perrin, 2003).

We based the design of the Talent Engagement Architect™ Survey upon all of the research. It assesses 11 factors of engagement:

A. Strategic Alignment
B. Trust in Senior Leadership
C. Immediate Manager Working Relationship
D. Peer Culture
E. Personal Influence
F. Nature of My Career
G. Career Support
H. Nature of the Job
I. Developmental Opportunities
J. Employee Recognition
K. Pay Fairness

These 11 factors are largely in an organization's control and are primary causes for the items identified in the Engagement Index. We refer to these 11 causes as *Engagement Drivers*. They represent key factors in organizations that influence the extent to which employees are engaged.

For a patient who receives test results indicating high blood pressure, high cholesterol levels, and obesity (the presenting symptoms), the remedies might include beginning a low-fat diet, quitting smoking, and starting an exercise regimen. Likewise, an organization that has low engagement levels indicated by scores on the items in the Engagement Index can look to remedies associated with the Engagement Drivers.

Some researchers assess the level of engagement by simply summing employees' scores of various drivers. Thus, an overall engagement score becomes the sum total of the drivers. We find that measuring engagement

6

like this is troublesome for two reasons. First, it is not really an assessment of engagement but rather an assessment of the causes of engagement (Schneider, 2006). Second, this approach does not reveal which of the drivers are having the greatest effect on engagement. Reporting survey results by driver and using a separate index of engagement enables management to determine which driver (or set of drivers) to change to make the greatest impact on engagement.

The following table represents the impact of one element of engagement on the next. The drivers are the primary causes of engagement. They are in the organization's control and the focus for efforts to enhance engagement. They affect attitudes and behaviors that are represented by the items in the Engagement Index. When those attitudes and behaviors are aligned with the organization, there will be positive outcomes that can be measured at the individual level. Collectively, those individual outcomes will have an impact on organizational outcomes that can also be measured.

Model of Employee Engagement

Engagement Drivers	Engagement Index	Individual Outcomes	Organizational Outcomes
• Strategic Alignment • Trust in Senior Leadership • Immediate Manager Working Relationship • Peer Culture • Personal Influence • Nature of My Career • Career Support • Nature of the Job • Developmental Opportunities • Employee Recognition • Pay Fairness	• Emotions *(energetic, inspiring, happy, satisfied, enthusiastic, passionate)* • Cognitions *(loyalty, ownership, trust, pride, support)* • Behaviors *(proactive, dedicated, motivated, personal initiative)*	• Turnover • Initiative • Extra effort • Seeking opportunities to contribute • Volunteering for assignments/ projects • Persistence • Receptive of organizational change • Satisfaction	• Productivity • Retention • Safety • Customer loyalty • Hiring savings • Training savings

7

The usefulness of engagement measurement and management relates to increased outcomes. Ultimately, the success of any engagement intervention or program translates into its return on investment. That determination starts by asking fundamental questions. Is the engagement level of the workforce increasing? Is it impacting individual and organizational outcomes? Are we deriving more financial benefits than we are spending?

Best Practices for Employee Engagement

Every organization must address engagement within the unique context created by its workforce, culture, and business conditions. The specific actions management takes to engage employees should be tailored to fit that context. But there are some best practices around employee engagement that apply to all organizations.

- **1. Align the workforce with business objectives.** Engagement drives discretionary behavior, but that's really only meaningful to the extent the behavior is aligned with the goals of the organization. Employee engagement needs to be aligned to create a competitive advantage for the organization (Dalal & Brummel, 2006). Behaviors that aren't aligned with organizational goals, even if otherwise benevolent and noble, shouldn't be considered engagement behaviors. To achieve alignment, ensure that the organization's vision, mission, values, and strategic objectives are clearly communicated to all employees. Everyone needs to know how their particular job contributes to the goals of the company.

- **2. Stick to a comprehensive plan.** It is a documented best practice to periodically conduct an engagement survey and share the results with employees. Based on survey results, action plans should be created and implemented, and the progress of those plans should be monitored (Bates, 2004). Be explicit in linking specific action items to survey data and don't neglect to follow through. Organizations that survey employees without sharing results and action items risk doing more harm than good.

- **3. Make line managers responsible for engagement.** Immediate supervisors and managers are the most crucial rung in the organizational ladder for increasing engagement. In many respects, these individuals define the job for the employee. They directly represent the organization's culture. They set expectations. They conduct performance appraisals and provide ongoing feedback. They decide who will have training opportunities. They determine workloads. They affect employees emotionally, cognitively, physically, behaviorally, and financially. The role of the front-line leader is of critical importance in building engagement (Frank, Finnegan, & Taylor, 2004).

- **4. Get commitment from senior management.** Line managers are likely the most important influencers of employee engagement. However, organizational leadership—the executive management team—also plays a

8

vital role. They steer the ship and set the tone. They allocate the resources. They mentor and coach line management on employee engagement issues. They resolve problems lower-level managers may not be able to address. Research on trust suggests that employees distinguish between direct leaders and upper authority levels when making assessments (Dirks & Ferrin, 2002). Employees who trust their organizational leaders will reciprocate in the form of loyalty, support, pride, and identity with the organization.

■ **5. Make Human Resources the owners of the process.** For employee engagement to be successful, HR must be at the center of the process. Best-in-class firms make HR the process owner ("How to succeed," 2004). HR manages the process, removes the barriers, and makes sure there is consistency of implementation. It is important that HR align the different personnel policies, practices, and systems to support employee engagement practices.

■ **6. Pay more attention to top talent.** It's important to engage all employees, but engaging high-potential talent is even more so. During the past several years, a growing number of executives have become concerned about their organization's ability to retain the best and brightest employees ("Avoiding the Brain Drain," 1999). The simple fact is that not all employees are of equal value to an organization. Top talent—the top performers and those with most potential—count most, and their loss hurts most. To maximize return on investment, spend the most time and resources on engaging the top talent. Organizations that identify high-potential employees early, carefully develop their careers, and reward them accordingly are much more likely to engage and retain them.

■ **7. Establish an organizational culture of engagement.** The traditional approach to employee engagement is to apply a fix-it method (Frank et al., 2004). Administer a survey, often in response to a perceived engagement problem. Diagnose the problem. Take action. Fix it. While the fix-it approach often leads to improvements, it's passive, piecemeal, and slow-moving. Better to be proactive, strategic, and dynamic. Employee engagement should be institutionalized—an integral part of the organization's culture rather than a tool that is only pulled out when something is broken. When employee engagement becomes ingrained in the culture, it creates and sustains the workforce (Corporate Leadership Council, 2004). High-performing companies are passionate about establishing a positive work environment (Hewitt Associates, 2004).

The best practices listed above apply to all organizations and form a foundation for other actions that can move the needle on employee engagement in your organization. Don't take them lightly.

You can't expect your employees to exceed the expectations of your customers
if you don't exceed the employees' expectations of management.
Howard Schultz – Chairman and CEO, Starbucks

Suggested Readings

Arthur, M. B., & Rousseau, D. M. (1996). *The boundaryless career: A new employment principle for a new organizational era.* NY: Oxford University Press.

Avoiding the brain drain: What companies are doing to lock in their talent. (1999, January). Kepner-Tregoe Research Monograph One.

Bates, S. (2004). Getting engaged. *HR Magazine, 49*(2), 44-51.

Bowling, N. A. (2007). Is the job satisfaction–job performance relationship spurious? A meta-analytic examination. *Journal of Vocational Behavior, 71,* 167-185.

Brown, S. P. (1996). A meta-analysis and review of organizational research on job involvement. *Psychological Bulletin, 120*(2), 235-256.

Collins, J. (2001). *Good to great.* NY: Harper Business.

Conger, J. A., & Kanungo, R. N. (1988). The empowerment process: Integrating theory and practice. *Academy of Management Review, 13,* 471-482.

Corporate Leadership Council. (2004). Driving performance and retention through employee engagement. Washington, DC: Author.

Dalal, R. S., & Brummel, B. J. (2006). *Understanding employee engagement: A discussion of the construct.* Panel Discussion at the Society for Industrial and Organizational Psychology Conference, Dallas.

De Meuse, K. P., & Tornow, W. W. (1990). The tie that binds – Has become very, very frayed! *Human Resource Planning, 13,* 203-213.

Dirks, K. T., & Ferrin, D. L. (2002). Trust in leadership: Meta-analytic findings and implications for research and practice. *Journal of Applied Psychology, 87,* 611-628.

Flade, P. (2003, December 11). Great Britain's workforce lacks inspiration. *Gallup Management Journal,* 1-3. Retrieved January 15, 2009, from www.gallup.com

Fleming, J. H., Coffman, C., & Harter, J. K. (2005). Manage your human sigma. *Harvard Business Review, 83*(7), 106-114.

Frank, F. D., Finnegan, R. P., & Taylor, C. R. (2004). The race for talent: Retaining and engaging workers in the 21st century. *Human Resource Planning, 27*(3), 12-24.

Gibbons, J. (2006). *Employee engagement: A review of current research and its implications.* New York: The Conference Board.

Hamel, G., & Breen, B. (2007). *The future of management.* Boston: MA: Harvard Business School Press.

Harter, J. K., Schmidt, F. L., & Hayes, T. L. (2002). Business-unit-level relationship between employee satisfaction, employee engagement, and business outcomes: A meta-analysis. *Journal of Applied Psychology, 87,* 268-279.

Hewitt Associates. (2004). *Research brief: Employee engagement higher at double-digit growth companies.* Retrieved January 15, 2009, from http://www.hewittassociates.com/_MetaBasicCMAssetCache_/Assets/Articles/DDGEngagementfull.pdf

How to succeed at succession plans. (2004, November). *HR Focus, 81*(11), 12-15.

Kabachnick, T. (2006). *I quit, but forgot to tell you: Attacking the spreading virus of disengagement.* Largo, FL: Kabachnick Group.

Kahn, W. A. (1990). Psychological conditions of personal engagement and disengagement at work. *Academy of Management Journal, 33,* 692-724.

Konrad, A. M. (2006). Engaging employees through high-involvement work practices. *Ivey Business Journal, 70*(4), 1-6.

Lockwood, N. R. (2007). Leveraging employee engagement for competitive advantage: HR's strategic role. *HR Magazine, 52*(3), 1-11.

Lodahl, T. M., & Kejner, M. (1965). The definition and measurement of job involvement. *Journal of Applied Psychology, 49,* 24-33.

Macey, W. H. (2007, April). *Disengagement, un-engagement, and misdirected engagement: Implications for the meaning of the engagement construct.* Paper presented at the Society for Industrial and Organizational Psychology Conference, New York.

Macey, W. H., & Schneider, B. (2008). The meaning of employee engagement. *Industrial and Organizational Psychology: Perspectives on Science and Practice, 1,* 3-30.

Mathieu, J. E., & Zajac, D. M. (1990). A review and meta-analysis of the antecedents, correlates, and consequences of organizational commitment. *Psychological Bulletin, 108,* 171–194.

Organ, D. W. (1988). *Organizational citizenship behavior: The good soldier syndrome.* Lexington, MA: D. C. Heath.

Pfau, B., & Kay, I. (2002). *The human capital edge.* NY: McGraw-Hill.

Reichheld, F. F. (2001). Lead for loyalty. *Harvard Business Review, 79*(7), 76-84.

Robinson, D., Perryman, S., & Hayday, S. (2004). *The drivers of employee engagement.* Brighton, UK: Institute for Employment Studies.

Rousseau, D. M. (1995). *Psychological contracts in organizations: Understanding written and unwritten agreements.* Thousand Oaks, CA: Sage.

Ryan, A. M., Schmit, M. J., & Johnson, R. (1996). Attitudes and effectiveness: Examining relations at an organizational level. *Personnel Psychology, 49,* 853-882.

Salanova, M., Agut, S., & Peiro, J. M. (2005). Linking organizational resources and work engagement to employee performance and customer loyalty: The mediation of service climate. *Journal of Applied Psychology, 90,* 1217-1227.

Schaufeli, W., Salanova, M., González-Romá, V., & Bakker, A. B. (2002). The measurement of engagement and burnout: A two sample confirmatory factor analytic approach. *Journal of Happiness Studies, 3,* 71-92.

Schippers, N. (2007). Retaining high potentials. *Talent Management, 3*(8), 38-41.

Schneider, B. (2006). Customer satisfaction. *Leadership Excellence, 23*(8), 13.

Sonnentag, S. (2003). Recovery, work engagement, and proactive behavior: A new look at the interface between nonwork and work. *Journal of Applied Psychology, 88*, 518-528.

Swindall, C. (2007). *Engaged leadership: Building a culture to overcome employee disengagement.* New Jersey: John Wiley & Sons, Inc.

Towers Perrin. (2003). *The 2003 Towers Perrin Talent Report: Working today: Understanding what drives employee engagement.* Retrieved January 15, 2009, from http://www.towersperrin.com/tp/getwebcachedoc?webc=HRS/USA/2003/200309/Talent_2003.pdf

Ulrich, D., Eichinger, R. W., Kulas, J. T., & De Meuse, K. P. (2007). *50 More things you need to know: The science behind best people practices for managers & HR professionals.* Minneapolis, MN: Lominger International: A Korn/Ferry Company.

Vance, R. J. (2006). *Effective practice guidelines: Employee engagement and commitment.* Alexandria, VA: SHRM Foundation.

Wiley, J. W. (2007). Employee engagement: What it does and does not give you. Paper presented in Practitioner Forum at the Society for Industrial and Organizational Psychology Conference, New York.

Wright, T. A., & Cropanzano, R. (2005). Psychological well-being and job satisfaction as predictors of job performance. *Journal of Occupational Health Psychology, 5*, 84-94.

Chapter 2
Engagement of High-Potential Talent

The kind of commitment I find among the best performers
across virtually every field is a single-minded passion
for what they do, an unwavering desire for excellence
in the way they think and the way they work.
Jim Collins – Management consultant and author

All employees are important. Some are more important than others. Generally, it's financially expedient to invest in retaining solid contributors and engaging every employee. But the stakes for engaging, developing, and retaining top talent are much higher (Schippers, 2007).

Research has found that the gap between high-performing employees and other employees is huge. For example, 50% of all books in the U.S. Library of Congress were written by 10% of published authors. Sixteen composers have produced half of all classical music. It has been shown that the best software engineers are at least 20 times more productive than the average engineers and 30 times more productive than the worst (Pfeffer & Sutton, 2006).

When such a high-potential, seasoned performer leaves the company, it creates a costly void. The leadership and performance of the firm can be impacted for years. A recent study conducted by the Society for Human Resource Management concluded the most critical challenge facing organizations today is finding and retaining the best talent (Allen, 2007). Another recent study performed by the Center for Creative Leadership found that talent acquisition and development was the most significant challenge confronting companies today (Martin, 2007).

Even if organizations are successful in recruiting top talent, they won't optimize that talent unless individuals are engaged and retained. And that's the focus of this chapter. An exclusive focus on high-potential talent. A focus on the people who will be primary drivers of sustainable and profitable growth in your organization. The employees on a fast track to a top leadership position. The employees you can least afford to lose to the competition.

Several major workplace trends complicate the task of engaging and retaining high-potential talent. Although many of the issues facing organizations and their leaders have been emerging over the past three decades, today's global economy magnifies their importance.

■ **1. The global economy has created a global workforce.** It used to be that a design engineer at Ford may be persuaded to work at GM or Chrysler if he/she was disappointed with his/her job. Nowadays, that Ford engineer might be swayed to Toyota, Mercedes, Volvo, Kia, Tata, or Geely. The open marketplace has created multiple job opportunities for motivated, talented, and ambitious employees. The most talented people have a multitude of options in the global economy. The most successful organizations attract talent at a higher rate with a well-established employment brand that has global reach. Once employed in those most successful organizations, top talent becomes fully engaged. And they aren't easily lured away by other opportunities.

■ **2. The aging and retirement of the global workforce.** Based on demographic trends, roughly 13% of U.S. workers are age 55 or older today, and this figure is expected to increase to 20% by 2015 (U.S. General Accounting Office, 2001). This fact is not limited to the United States. For example, in the United Kingdom, 30% of the workforce currently is over age 50 (Dixon, 2003). Countries in the European Union project the number of employees over age 50 to increase to nearly 25% by 2020 ("Turning boomers into boomerangs," 2006). And 41% of the Canadian workforce is projected to be between the ages of 45 and 64 by 2021 (Lende, 2005). The labor pool is shrinking. The competition for the remaining employees who are deemed more talented will become even fiercer in the near future.

■ **3. The decline of managerial positions in the organizational hierarchy.** Organizations continue to flatten. Corporate restructuring and downsizing have led to fewer layers of management in many organizations. At one time, talented individuals would be promoted every couple of years as they climbed the organizational hierarchy from lower, to middle, and then to upper management. As companies removed these opportunities for vertical promotions to enhance efficiency and reduce labor costs, a side effect was more difficulty retaining talented employees who defined career success in terms of upward advancement.

■ **4. A frequent disconnect between employee pay and organizational contribution.** Many and possibly most organizations claim to use, or at least aspire to use, a pay-for-performance strategy. A survey administered in a wide variety of companies asked managers to identify the typical difference in contribution between a below-average employee and a top-level employee in the same pay grade. The average response: over 100%. When these same managers were asked to identify the typical pay difference between high and low performers, their response was: between 5% and 10% (see Goldsmith, Greenberg, Robertson, & Hu-Chan, 2003). Accurate discrimination of performance and differential rewards for high and low performers only occur in organizations that have courageous managers, fully supportive top management, and an aligned organizational culture. The internal inequities created in organizations that don't discriminate performance and differentially reward talent are valid reasons for top performers to leave. Why shouldn't they look for another firm that will fairly reward them for their contributions?

■ **5. Reduced status of working in large corporations.** Historically, the college graduate's dream job was in a big company, a job with a good starting salary, great benefits, lots of opportunities for advancement, and job security. Those dream jobs began drying up in the downsizing era of the 1980s and 1990s as large Fortune 500 companies began implementing wave after wave of downsizing to reduce levels of middle management and streamline bureaucratic practices (De Meuse & Marks, 2003). For many college grads, the focus shifted to finding jobs in smaller, entrepreneurial, high-tech start-ups that promised a fast-paced, challenging environment and stock options. This is especially true for the most talented employees who are often quick to trade stability and security for challenge, risk, excitement, and the potential of outsized financial rewards.

■ **6. The rise of the knowledge worker.** In today's workplace, intellectual capital is the most important asset in most firms. Bill Gates recently said that Microsoft will do whatever it takes to hire and retain the brightest and best software designers on the planet. As the value of key knowledge workers increases, the competition to attract and retain those employees continues to intensify.

■ **7. The proliferation of mergers and acquisitions (M&A).** Even in times of a weaker economy, merger activity continues. Depressed stock prices and foreign exchange rates make for some attractive purchases. M&A activity frequently results in downsizing, which creates employee apprehension, anxiety, and fear. The employees that these newly merged companies can least afford to lose are often the first to go—the talented ones who have lots of options. To make matters worse, other companies not involved in the M&A often actively recruit the most talented workers (Bastien, Hostager, & Miles, 1996).

■ **8. Erosion of the traditional employer/employee relationship.** In 1956, William H. Whyte published a fascinating little book titled *The Organization Man*. In this book, Whyte described a business world where the employee was completely invested in the company, working 50-hour weeks, volunteering for overtime at every turn, and relocating the family on a minute's notice. In return, the corporation provided a good job with good pay and benefits, gave annual pay raises, and offered ample opportunity for advancement. It was a cradle-to-grave mentality (De Meuse & Tornow, 1990; Rousseau, 1995). Such workplaces are virtually extinct in most parts of the world. The old, simple, and paternalistic employer/employee relationship of stability, order, and predictability has been replaced. The new work world is weaving a dynamic relationship based on self-reliance, independence, and reciprocity which accommodates diversity of all types and integrates a mosaic of heritages, ethnicities, values, and individual differences. This evolving new work agreement brings with it new roles, responsibilities, and opportunities for each party. The necessity to fully engage employees, particularly high-potential employees, becomes more difficult under these new rules since employee loyalty and job security are less guaranteed today (De Meuse & Marks, 2003; Morris, 2006).

The competitive landscape has changed. And so have attitudes toward work. The intangible value contributed by human capital has risen dramatically for most organizations over the past 30 years (Weatherly, 2003). A disproportionate share of that intangible human capital value is provided by a handful of employees in most firms. Organizations that effectively deal with these workplace dynamics are proactively developing talent management systems to identify, attract, engage, and retain the best people.

Design and Development of the Talent Engagement Architect™ Survey

There are many satisfactory general employee surveys on the market. Our goal was to create an instrument that did more than assess general levels of engagement. We wanted to also be able to distinguish the views and needs of high-potential talent.

We hypothesized that because high potentials approach their work differently, they are also likely to be engaged differently than the rest of the employee population. That they value certain work characteristics more or less than other employees. That they need challenging assignments more than others. We know that high potentials are more marketable and have more employment options. If special efforts aren't taken to fully engage them, they are more likely to quickly leave an organization.

In an article entitled "Retaining High Impact Performers," Goldsmith (1996) reported on surveys of "highest potential future leaders." He defined this type of employee as one who could obtain another job with a pay raise with very little effort. The following six factors were identified as key to retaining them: (1) showing respect and dignity; (2) creating an organizational environment where employees can continue to develop and grow; (3) providing ongoing training and developmental opportunities; (4) coaching and mentoring employees; (5) providing ongoing feedback on the personal level; and (6) rewarding and recognizing others' achievements. As amazing as it may seem, when high-potential employees were asked why they left a company, many revealed that no one had ever asked them to stay (Goldsmith et al., 2003).

Our focus has been on developing a survey instrument that goes beyond assessing general levels of employee engagement to provide practical, specific help for organizations to engage and retain high-potential talent. The most effective organizations have learned to aggressively manage human assets with a level of rigor that rivals that devoted to managing financial assets. The Talent Engagement Architect™ Survey was developed to facilitate this level of rigor around managing high-potential talent.

How Our Survey Was Developed

Research has shown that one of the primary predictors of being classified as a high-potential employee is learning agility. Several authors have found a direct link between employee potential and scores on a learning agility assessment (e.g., Church & Desrosiers, 2006; Connolly & Viswesvaran, 2002; Lombardo & Eichinger, 2000; Spreitzer, McCall, & Mahoney, 1997).

To develop the Talent Engagement Architect™ Survey, we administered both this survey and the Choices Architect® Survey (Lominger's validated assessment of learning agility; see Lombardo & Eichinger, 2000) to groups of employees from several companies across different industries. We then correlated each of the items on the Talent Engagement Architect™ Survey with individual scores on the Choices Architect® Survey. In addition, we correlated each of the items on the Talent Engagement Architect™ Survey with the following two measures of intention to voluntarily separate from the current organization: (1) I am thinking about leaving this company; and (2) I am actively seeking to leave this company.

The analyses showed that high potentials were especially sensitive to some (but not all) of the items on our engagement survey. Those special items align with four distinct factors of high-potential engagement, and specific items embedded in our Talent Engagement Architect™ Survey directly assess these four factors. We refer to the factors as *Hi-Po Drivers* because they drive engagement for high-potential employees. Thus, our engagement survey can be used to measure engagement for the general workforce as a whole, as well as to assess the level of engagement of a company's high-potential talent.

Our research led us to discover that high-potential employees are indeed engaged somewhat differently than other employees. Initial findings suggest that high-potential individuals who do not score substantially (one standard deviation) above the mean of other employees in the organization on the items that comprise the Hi-Po Drivers are at risk of leaving.

How the Assessment Works

The Talent Engagement Architect™ Survey is scored twice. First, the survey is scored for all employees like any other engagement survey. Second, it is rescored for those individuals who have been identified as having high potential. The scores on the four Hi-Po Driver factors are analyzed to contrast responses between the two employee groups. If the scores of high-potential employees on those items are not at least one standard deviation higher than the workforce in general, it is an indication of problems with high-potential engagement.

Differential Treatment for Top Talent – A Focus on the Hi-Po Drivers

High potentials live in the future. Although they are performing well today, they also are concerned about where they will be and what they will be doing in the future. They are selective and demanding. They have many career options, and they know it. They have significant market value. They regularly receive calls from search consultants and unsolicited opportunities. On one hand, our studies show that high potentials value many workplace characteristics in the same way as the general employee population. They are concerned about many of the same aspects of their jobs, bosses, and the organizational culture as is everyone else. On the other hand, they are particularly sensitive to the four Hi-Po Drivers. Whether they decide to stay and complete their career in their current organization or leave for another opportunity largely depends on these factors.

What It Means for Your Organization

Jobs, in general, are increasing in responsibility and difficulty as organizations continue to grow more complex, dynamic, and international in scope. Ironically, at the same time, the supply of talent is shrinking dramatically due to demographic realities. In this perfect storm, traditional methods for talent assessment and development are simply not enough. Competition for talent makes it imperative for organizations to aggressively take steps to fully engage employees, especially those with high potential.

Assessing and improving engagement in your entire workforce can make a significant difference to the success of your organization. Specifically assessing and enhancing high-potential engagement can raise organizational performance to a whole new level.

You can never have enough talent.
Pat Riley – Legendary basketball coach

Suggested Readings

Allen, D. G. (2007). *Retaining talent: A guide to analyzing and managing employee turnover*. Alexandria, VA: Society for Human Resource Management.

The Art & Science of Talent. (2007). News release. Los Angeles: Korn/ Ferry International. Retrieved from: http://ir.kornferry.com/phoenix. zhtml?c=100800&p=irol-newsArticle&ID=1128020&highlight=

Bastien, D. T., Hostager, T. J., & Miles, H. H. (1996). Corporate judo: Exploiting the dark side of change when competitors merge, acquire, downsize, or restructure. *Journal of Management Inquiry, 5*, 261-275.

Bradt, G., Check, J. A., & Pedraza, J. (2006). *The new leader's 100-day action plan*. Hoboken, NJ: John Wiley & Sons.

Church, A. H., & Desrosiers, E. I. (2006, April). *Talent management: Will the high potentials please stand up*. Symposium presented at the Society for Industrial and Organizational Psychology Conference, Dallas.

Collins, J. (2001). *Good to great*. NY: Harper Business.

Connolly, J. A., & Viswesvaran, C. (2002, April). *Assessing the construct validity of a measure of learning agility*. Research paper presented at the Society for Industrial and Organizational Psychology Conference, Toronto.

De Meuse, K. P., & Marks, M. L. (2003). *Resizing the organization: Managing layoffs, divestitures, and closings*. San Francisco: Jossey-Bass.

De Meuse, K. P., & Tornow, W. W. (1990). The tie that binds – Has become very, very frayed. *Human Resource Planning, 13*, 203-213.

Dixon, S. (2003). Implications of population ageing for the labour market. *Labour Market Trends, 111*(2), 67-76.

Effron, M., Salob, M., & Greenslade, S. (2005). *Research highlights: How the top 20 companies grow great leaders*. Lincolnshire, IL: Hewitt.

Goldsmith, M. (1996, Summer). Retaining high-impact performers. *Leader to Leader Journal* (Premier Issue).

Goldsmith, M., Greenberg, C. L., Robertson, A., & Hu-Chan, M. (2003). *Global leadership: The next generation*. Upper Saddle River, NJ: Prentice Hall Financial Times.

Houlihan, P. (2008, February 29). The human capitalist: Five minutes with Gary Becker. *Chicago GSP Magazine*.

Lende, T. (2005). Older workers: Opportunity or challenge? *Canadian Manager, 30*(1), 20-20.

Lombardo, M. M., & Eichinger, R. W. (2000). High potentials as high learners. *Human Resource Management, 39*, 321-329.

Martin, A. (2007). *What's next? The 2007 Changing nature of leadership survey*. Greensboro, NC: Center for Creative Leadership.

Morris, B. (2006, July 24). The new rules. *Fortune, 154*(2), 70-87.

2

Peterson, D. B. (2002). Management development: Coaching and mentoring program. In K. Kraiger (Ed.), *Creating, implementing, and managing effective training and development.* San Francisco: Jossey-Bass.

Pfeffer, J., & Sutton, R. I. (2006). Hard facts, *dangerous half-truths and total nonsense: Profiting from evidence-based management.* Boston, MA: Harvard Business School Press.

Rousseau, D. M. (1995). *Psychological contracts in organizations: Understanding written and unwritten agreements.* Thousand Oaks, CA: Sage.

Schippers, N. (2007). Retaining high potentials. *Talent Management, 3*(8), 38-41.

Spreitzer, G. M., McCall, M. W., & Mahoney, J. D. (1997). Early identification of international executive potential. *Journal of Applied Psychology, 82,* 6-20.

Turning boomers into boomerangs. (2006, February 16). *Economist, 378,* 65-67.

U.S. General Accounting Office. (2001). *Older workers: Demographic trends pose challenges for employers and workers.* Washington, DC: Author.

Weatherly, L. (2003). The value of people: The challenges and opportunities of human capital measurement and reporting. *Society for Human Resource Management Research Quarterly*, Vol. 3.

Whyte, W. H., Jr. (1956). *The organization man.* New York: Simon & Schuster.

2

Engagement Driver A
Strategic Alignment

The best CEOs I know are teachers,
and at the core of what they teach is strategy.
Michael Porter – Author and Professor of Management and Economics

The Signpost

The best business strategy is only so much fluff if not executed well. So, how will you execute that great strategy? Can you do it without an engaged workforce? Almost certainly not. Your employees need to understand where the business is going and how it's going to get there. Your employees need to see agreement—alignment—between your strategy, the values you promote, and your behavior.

Unskilled

- ☐ Can't craft a compelling vision
- ☐ Doesn't understand the business landscape, the market, the competition
- ☐ Is not totally clear about the mission and purpose of the business
- ☐ Plans ineffectively; creates plans that aren't realistic and actionable
- ☐ Holds information close to the vest
- ☐ Doesn't achieve clarity; messages are disorganized or ambiguous
- ☐ Fails to deliver communication in a timely manner
- ☐ Compromises on talent; makes do with less than the best
- ☐ Does not hold people accountable
- ☐ Doesn't make decisions aligned with the strategy

Skilled

- ☐ Communicates a clear, compelling vision
- ☐ Creates a focused strategy aligned with customers and organizational capabilities
- ☐ Maintains an intimate connection with customers and acts on feedback
- ☐ Closely monitors competitors and knows their strategies
- ☐ Establishes metrics and reward systems that measure and reinforce the strategic intent
- ☐ Aims for clarity of purpose and straightforward, candid messages
- ☐ Provides timely and relevant information to all who need it

A

- ☐ Has an eye for talent and selects the very best people for the role
- ☐ Drives the message about competitive strategy to every corner of the organization
- ☐ Makes investment decisions based upon the strategy

Some Causes

- ☐ Lack of strategic focus and clarity
- ☐ Silos and organizational barriers to communication
- ☐ Narrow perspective
- ☐ Unorganized
- ☐ Lack of communication skills
- ☐ Poor time management
- ☐ Leader defensiveness
- ☐ Complacency
- ☐ Insufficient focus on talent management
- ☐ Lack of managerial courage

The Ten Leadership Architect® Competencies Most Associated with This Engagement Driver *(in order of connectedness)*

2. *Dealing with* Ambiguity
5. Business Acumen
58. Strategic Agility
47. Planning
50. Priority Setting
12. Conflict Management
25. Hiring and Staffing
36. Motivating Others
46. Perspective
65. *Managing* Vision and Purpose

The Map

Misalignment is easy to detect. Strategic goals. Mission statements. Vision statements. Core values statements. Leader behaviors. Organizational capabilities. Policies and procedures. People practices. When there is misalignment of any of these key factors, your people will spot it in a minute. Misalignment creates confusion, breeds mistrust, and generally leads to malaise. On the other hand, alignment creates a sense of purpose and generates energy as everyone senses they're pulling in the same direction. Keep employees informed of organization-relevant information to increase ownership, buy-in, engagement, and commitment to the organization and its goals. Communicate frequently

22

to ensure that employees know what the organization is doing and why at all times. Reinforce the guiding principles found in your mission, strategy, and values statements frequently. These are keys to driving organizational decisions and almost impossible to overcommunicate. Employees kept in the loop feel valued and are more likely to work toward collective goals. Employees shouldn't be surprised by company decisions and actions. Employees with a common mind-set based upon timely and accurate information will act in concert with greater efficiency and effectiveness. And that leads to execution. Even great strategies that are well communicated are doomed without follow-through and execution. Create a common mind-set in your organization so everyone knows what the strategy is and what tactics and plans to follow. Every employee should be able to clearly explain the strategy in a couple of sentences. They should be able to explain how they contribute to the strategy. When everyone can do that, you'll have achieved a common mind-set; you'll have reduced friction in your processes and increased the efficiency of decision making, resource allocation, and initiatives. And you'll have bolstered the confidence of the workforce in the mission and leadership. A confident workforce pulling in one direction is an engaged workforce.

Some Remedies

☐ **1. Craft compelling mission, vision, and values statements.** Do you have a good story to tell? A story told with vivid language? A story that starts with the customer and clearly describes how your organization will delight the customer? Can you tell that story concisely, in just a few words? When you can, you've got your mission. And what's the next chapter in your story, the story that describes the future? Begin by stepping back and seeing the big picture. Look to the future. Three years. Five years. Ten years. Create a shared vision. What will be different? The same? Be specific. Get people together and take time to discuss the vision. Pull out varying perspectives. Take time to wordsmith a compact description that paints a memorable picture of the future. When you've got that, you've got your vision. Now, what do you care about? What do you value? What are the attributes that you want to promote in your leadership? In your workforce? Think seriously about this. Don't take it lightly. And don't be a Pollyanna about it by selecting values through the lens of political correctness. Identify only the values that you really will exemplify, reward, and promote at every opportunity. They should be few in number. And each one should be easily linked to the mission and vision.

☐ **2. Create a compelling business strategy.** Your mission, vision, and values statements provide the context to continue the story, to frame your strategy. The strategy is your roadmap for making your vision a reality. A compelling business strategy starts with the customer. It puts meat on the bones of the mission statement. A compelling strategy starkly contrasts your organization with the competition. It is easily understood. It engages all stakeholders—customers, investors, and the workforce. It's bold. Challenging. It defines what it is that your organization will do better than any other. It clearly spells out your value proposition. And it plays to your core organizational capabilities. The business strategy should be something that everyone in the organization can sink their teeth into. Something that provides guidance and focus for effort, resource allocation, decision making, and behaviors.

☐ **3. Clearly communicate the strategy, vision, mission, and values to employees.** Choose your words carefully. Create a shared vocabulary that is used consistently in all messages around strategy, mission, vision, and values. Talk the talk. Reinforce the message and vocabulary at every opportunity. We think with words. A common language is critical to arriving at a shared understanding in the organization. Be consistent in using that language. And use it often. It's nearly impossible to overcommunicate about strategy, mission, vision, and values if you're using focused and targeted communications. Doing so will promote buy-in, commitment, and involvement around the business strategy. When everyone is on the same page in the playbook, there is less friction, more efficiency, greater engagement.

☐ **4. Ensure that employees understand and support the strategy and adopt the values.** Put as much effort into communicating strategy and values to the workforce as you do in designing a key ad campaign to reach customers. Craft the message by carefully considering the audience and purpose. What important information do employees need to understand the strategy? To align their efforts to the strategy? To do their jobs effectively? Engage an internal or external PR staff member to help create key messages. Establish context around the message. How was the strategy created? Where did the values come from? Why are they important? How will they help us achieve our mission? What's the competition doing? How will you respond? How will accomplishments be measured? How were objectives and goals set? Who is accountable for what? What are the rewards and consequences for excellent performance? Where are the resources? What is the best way to get things done? Who can I ask for help? Use as many media and channels as practical to communicate. Employ new communication technologies effectively. Create an employee Web site. Videos. Special forums for information sharing. Information lunches. Newsletters. Build internal communication channels. Hold all leaders accountable for teaching, for explaining, for modeling, and for rewarding the right behaviors.

☐ **5. Define talent requirements for strategic execution in terms of competencies.** You can think about your organization as bundles of capabilities—your core competencies at the organization level. To a large extent, these organizational-level capabilities are comprised of the sum of the individual competencies that exist in your workforce. Organizational capabilities embody the knowledge and skills of an organization; they're the things that your firm does well or perhaps not so well. They predict what strategies are likely to be successful. It follows, then, that you need to clearly understand the organizational capabilities required to give you a competitive advantage and lead to successful implementation of your strategy. Your board of directors should, of course, be involved in creating your strategy. A good board will have a wealth of experience with several organizations, including yours, and can inject a fresh perspective to planning that can pierce through groupthink. Just as important, your board and top leadership team should be involved in identifying critical organizational capabilities. And don't stop there. Drill down from organizational capabilities to the specific leadership competencies that will define success for your firm. Every strategy, given a particular industry context, location, and market, has a set of required leadership skills and competencies. A strategy that calls for speed in decision making needs speedy managers and executives. A strategy that calls for key account intimacy requires managers and executives who are good at forming lasting relationships. A strategy that calls for producing commodity products in a cost-conscious market needs leaders who are efficient managers. For each element of the strategy, consider what kind of leader or manager will best be able to execute this element. Define your leadership requirements in terms of competencies. Competencies give you the vocabulary, the precise language you need to define talent requirements. And you can't manage the talent proposition unless you're clear about the requirements. Competency success profiles that are aligned with your strategy will provide focus for a broad spectrum of talent processes—selection, development, deployment, and succession.

☐ **6. Assess current competency levels of your workforce.** You can't fully understand the strength of your leadership team, of your bench strength, without assessment. It's important to regularly assess your workforce in the key competencies in the success profile. Begin at the top level. Conduct objective, accurate assessments of the current leadership competencies of your senior management team. The critical role of top leadership warrants external assessments by certified assessors, often psychologists. Useful assessment tools include behavioral interviews, situational judgment tests, simulations, measures of work style, and 360° feedback instruments. Don't stop with the leadership, though. Competency gaps in your highly leveraged key performers can undermine your strategy. If any part of the value chain requires skillful execution for the strategy to succeed, carefully check the talent requirements for the people who impact that part of the business. Create an assessment program for the top three levels in your organization.

Assess each person against the competencies you have identified as critical for success. And get your managers engaged in working with individuals to create personalized development plans to fill gaps.

☐ **7. Acquire talent strategically from outside the organization.** It takes time to develop competencies, and if the competencies needed to execute your strategy aren't sufficient in your current workforce, time will work against you. In that case, you will likely need to consider hiring or partnering with the talent that will give you a competitive advantage and enable execution of your strategy. Use objective, validated assessment methods when selecting talent to get the best fit and avoid the costs of derailment and rehiring. For long-term competitive advantage, you'll need to internalize the ability to build competencies that are in short supply and not easily replicated by your competitors. In the short-run, though, hiring from the outside can kick-start your talent management efforts. Hiring from the outside can also be used judiciously over the long-term to ensure that fresh ideas and energy are injected into the talent pipeline.

☐ **8. Develop internal talent strategically.** Align your learning and development function with your business strategy by addressing the gaps in your core leadership competencies, the competencies that will drive your strategy. Make those competencies the centerpiece of training and development in the organization. Develop instruction around the systems and processes created to optimize execution of your strategy. Teach analytical methods. Teach the business drivers for your organization. Teach problem-solving and decision-making techniques and involve employees in action-learning projects with real implications. Be realistic, though, about the limitations of training. Most competency gaps can only be partially addressed by training. People learn most of what they know by doing on the job and by working with others. Look to development activities such as special assignments to complete the picture. Design developmental opportunities to strengthen skills in strategy. Assign managers and key employees to organizational committees, task forces, and special projects for development. Employ action learning to get managers involved in solving real business problems while they collaborate and learn. Senior managers and board members should mentor, coach, and evaluate solutions created by project teams. Look for extracurricular learning activities that teach and reinforce strategic thinking—activities such as serving on the board of a nonprofit or professional organization. And don't neglect the transfer of training back to the job. It's critical to ensure that what's learned in training and development is retained and applied on the job. Managers and supervisors must be involved in the transfer of training to make sure that people have opportunities to apply what they've learned and receive feedback on their performance.

☐ **9. Ensure that all talent management practices are aligned with the business strategy.** It's not enough to create a great competitive strategy. You need alignment. Your people must understand and share a common view of the future. They must share commitment to the strategic goals. Bring a laser-like focus to aligning everything to your strategy. Your processes. Your organizational structure. Policies. Procedures. Compensation and rewards. Hiring. Performance management. Succession planning. Decision making. Communication. Everything focused on achieving your competitive business strategy. Ensure that your top-level business goals accurately capture your strategic intent. From the top of the organization, those goals should cascade down to the individual employee. Every individual contributor should have goals aligned with and in support of the team. The team goals should be aligned with and in support of the department, and so forth. From the top of the organization to the bottom, establish goals so people and groups are aligned with the strategy. Goals, measurement, and feedback—all are essential to align and engage the workforce. And make sure to align your reward system to your strategies to reinforce the behaviors, accomplishments, and skill development that will drive competitive advantage and success.

☐ **10. Define and implement key measures of talent management practices.** You can't manage without measurement. Measurement gets people's attention. Starting with your highest level strategic objectives, break them down into measurable, actionable goals that address each of the four quadrants of a balanced scorecard. In your employee quadrant, use meaningful, results-based measurements that capture a variety of talent management effectiveness criteria tied to your strategy. The measures should provide answers to important questions related to issues such as engagement levels in the workforce, the depth and robustness of your talent pipeline, retention of talent, diversity trends, effectiveness of learning and development, deployment of talent into key jobs, movement of high-potential talent between business units, and completion of robust development plans.

I like to tell people that all of our products and business will go through three phases. There's vision, patience, and execution.
Steve Ballmer – CEO, Microsoft

Suggested Readings

Aaker, D. A. (2001). *Developing business strategies* (6th ed.). NY: John Wiley & Sons.

Abraham, G. A. (2006). Strategic alignment. *Leadership Excellence, 23*(8), 12.

Allio, M. K. (2005). A short, practical guide to implementing strategy. *Journal of Business Strategy, 26*(4), 12-21.

Bossidy, L., & Charan, R. (2002). *Execution: The discipline of getting things done.* NY: Crown Business.

Bradford, R. (2002). Strategic alignment. *Executive Excellence, 19*(1), 8-9.

Branham, F. L. (2001). *Keeping the people who keep you in business: 24 Ways to hang on to your most valuable talent.* NY: AMACOM.

Christensen, C. M., Roth, E. A., & Anthony, S. D. (2004). *Seeing what's next: Using theories of innovation to predict industry change.* Boston, MA: Harvard Business School Press.

Eichinger, R. W., Ruyle, K. E., & Ulrich, D. O. (2007). *FYI for strategic effectiveness™.* Minneapolis, MN: Lominger International: A Korn/Ferry Company.

Goodstein, L. D., Nolan, T. M., & Pfeiffer, J. W. (1993). *Applied strategic planning: A comprehensive guide.* New York: McGraw-Hill, Inc.

Kaplan, R. S., & Norton, D. P. (2001). Building a strategy-focused organization. *Ivey Business Journal, 65*(5), 12-19.

Kaplan, R. S., & Norton, D. P. (2006). How to implement a new strategy without disrupting your organization. *Harvard Business Review, 84*(3), 100.

Kim, W. C., & Mauborgne, R. (2005). *Blue ocean strategy: How to create uncontested market space and make competition irrelevant.* Boston, MA: Harvard Business School Press.

Lawler, E. E., III. (1997). *From the ground up: Six principles for building the new logic corporation.* San Francisco: Jossey-Bass.

Levin, I. M. (2000). Vision revisited: Telling the story of the future. *Journal of Applied Behavioral Science, 36*, 91-107.

Lewis, C. P. (1997). *Building a shared vision: A leader's guide to aligning the organization.* Portland, OR: Productivity Press.

Maccoby, M. (2003). *The productive narcissist: The promise and peril of visionary leadership.* NY: Broadway Books.

Mintzberg, H., Ahlstrand, B. W., & Lampel, J. (2005). *Strategy bites back: It is a lot more, and less, than you ever imagined.* Upper Saddle River, NJ: Pearson Prentice Hall.

Porter, M. E. (1998a). *Competitive advantage: Creating and sustaining superior performance.* NY: Free Press.

Porter, M. E. (1998b). *Competitive strategy: Techniques for analyzing industries and competitors.* NY: Free Press.

Senge, P. M. (1990). *The fifth discipline: The art & practice of the learning organization.* NY: Doubleday Currency.

Smith, J. L., & Flanagan, W. G. (2006). *Creating competitive advantage: Give your customers a reason to choose you over your competitors.* NY: Doubleday Currency.

Ulwick, A. (2005). *What customers want: Using outcome-driven innovation to create breakthrough products and services.* NY: McGraw-Hill.

Williams, S. L. (2002). Strategic planning and organizational values: Links to alignment. *Human Resource Development International, 5*(2), 217-233.

Engagement Driver B
Trust in Senior Leadership

I think if you look at people, whether in business or government,
who haven't had any moral compass, who've just changed
to say whatever they thought the popular thing was,
in the end they're losers.
Michael Bloomberg – Founder, Bloomberg Financial Media Company
and Mayor of New York City

The Signpost

Trust. Hard to win. Easy to lose. And so critical to engaging your workforce. Your people want to be proud of their leaders. To believe in them. To trust them. To follow them. Your people don't want to hear fairy tales, to have the truth softened by leaders who are uncomfortable in conflict or unwilling to take the heat. They want to hear the truth from courageous leaders who earn trust and show trust in others.

Unskilled

- ☐ Communicates guardedly, only on a "need to know" basis
- ☐ Fails to accept criticism; defensive; punitive
- ☐ Tolerates or supports double standards for executives and others
- ☐ Fails to identify, communicate, and model core organizational values
- ☐ Shrouds decision making in secrecy; process is exclusive rather than inclusive
- ☐ Glosses over difficult issues; spins all news positively
- ☐ Fails to accept responsibility, shifts blame when things go wrong; hogs credit when things go right
- ☐ Makes frequent managerial missteps that damage credibility
- ☐ Maintains distance from general employee population; is isolated, inaccessible, out of touch
- ☐ Tolerates and excuses unprincipled behavior and cronyism
- ☐ Doesn't create communication channels that promote upward flow of information
- ☐ Fails to demonstrate care and concern for employees; lacks compassion

B

Skilled

- ☐ Frequently speaks about core organizational values; takes time to explain and promote them
- ☐ Consistently models speech and behavior aligned with core values
- ☐ Manages skillfully; demonstrates thorough understanding of the business and competitive landscape
- ☐ Deals fairly with others; doesn't tolerate double standards or favoritism
- ☐ Actively seeks input from all parts of the organization; welcomes diversity of opinion
- ☐ Is visible; gets out of the office to establish a personal presence and connection with the workforce
- ☐ Exercises the highest practical level of transparency and inclusion in decision making; explains how and why decisions are made
- ☐ Demonstrates good intentions through actions as well as words; doesn't keep secret agendas
- ☐ Freely shares information; engages in straight talk; doesn't dance around issues and backpedal when there is bad news
- ☐ Practices an open-door policy; listens attentively and follows up
- ☐ Quickly gives credit where credit is due; gladly steps out of the spotlight to provide room for others
- ☐ Is accountable; accepts responsibility without playing the martyr when things go poorly

Some Causes

- ☐ Unclear about vision and values
- ☐ Failure to listen
- ☐ Lack of business acumen
- ☐ Arrogance; hubris
- ☐ History of tension, disputes, controversy, or scandal
- ☐ Favoritism; nepotism
- ☐ Rigid hierarchical organizational structure; silo mentality
- ☐ Narcissism; egomania
- ☐ Insecurity; fear of loss of control
- ☐ Us vs. them mentality

B

The Ten Leadership Architect® Competencies Most Associated with This Engagement Driver *(in order of connectedness)*

12. Conflict Management
29. Integrity and Trust
33. Listening
 9. Command Skills
20. Directing Others
23. Fairness to Direct Reports
34. Managerial Courage
 2. *Dealing with* Ambiguity
 3. Approachability
36. Motivating Others

The Map

It takes a long time to build a fortune by putting a penny per day in a piggybank. Smash the bank and you've got to start over—new bank and one penny at a time. Trust is like that. It's hard-earned and steadily built over time but can be destroyed in an instant. Fortunately, research clearly indicates that most executives are rated high in trust and integrity. That's the good news. The bad news is that when trust is betrayed, the impact can be unpredictable and far-reaching. In some cases, trust that's lost can never be restored. Research studies validate what we would intuitively expect—trust in senior leadership has a significant impact on the engagement of the workforce. Trust inspires commitment. Trust promotes retention. Trust greases the wheels of organizational change. And the ways to build trust are easy to understand and supported by research studies. We trust leaders who are consistent, competent, fair, and show good intentions. Senior leaders have long been held to the highest standards. Rightly so. But it's becoming increasingly difficult for senior leaders to avoid problems with trust. Business conditions seem to shift more rapidly with every business cycle. The scale and global scope of many organizations continue to expand, and with that expansion comes more responsibility, increased ambiguity, and greater opportunities for missteps. The regulatory climate has resulted in much more transparency and requirements for disclosure. Missteps by leadership are subjected to the bright light of regulatory scrutiny. And the media tend to seize on bad news and disseminate it widely. As scale and global scope of operations expand, the demands on senior leadership also make it more difficult to stay in touch with the workforce, to put forward a personal face and model those things that build trust. In the absence of firsthand knowledge, employees are bound to make assumptions about isolated leadership. Assumptions lead to rumors

B

that can take on a life of their own and find their way into employee blogs that get read not only by employees in all corners of the organization, but by customers and investors. And whether right or wrong, rumors universally have a negative impact on trust. There's so much at stake. Leaders who take the issue of trust seriously—who guard it zealously and use every opportunity to build it—those are leaders who successfully impact engagement levels in their organization.

Some Remedies

☐ **1. Ensure that the management ranks are credible.** Trust starts with credibility. With competence. Shun incompetence like the plague. Eradicate it from your firm. Incompetent managers are perceived as goats by the workforce, the butt of jokes in comics and sitcoms. Fortunately, most managers aren't incompetent. But some are. Weed them out. Take this seriously. Assess your management ranks to ensure they have the core management skills to perform effectively: business acumen, functional/technical skills, directing others, priority setting, organizing, planning, time management, managing and measuring work, and so on. Pay special attention to delegation. A leader can't earn trust until it's given, and delegation is a primary way to demonstrate trust. Good delegators turn loose of complete tasks. They make assignments, ensure that the performer understands expectations, and then get out of the way, only intervening when required to remove roadblocks. Of course, good managers monitor progress and provide feedback and coaching along the way, but the intent is always to allow the employee to complete the task with as little unplanned support as possible. Insist that your management team proves its worth. Root out complacency, outmoded technical skills, and absentee management. These and other transgressions erode confidence and weaken the bonds of trust. Find the most glaring signs of underperformance and tackle them aggressively. Make it a team effort. Expect your leadership team, including all managers, to hold each other accountable. Competent management with a heavy dose of delegation is a primary way to build trust in the workforce.

☐ **2. Recognize and reinforce behaviors aligned with core values.** Trust starts with credibility but is bolstered with consistency. Walk the talk. A trite phrase perhaps, but nonetheless enormously important when it comes to building trust. Without consistency, trust flies out the window. If people perceive that leaders' actions are not in line with what they are saying, they simply won't be trusted. Even small, unintentional gaps and inconsistencies chip away at trust. It's not enough to be on the mark just some of the time. Consistency is key. So what's your message? Are

B

you communicating core values that are consistent and aligned with the organization's mission and vision? Are the core values non-negotiable? Are your leaders modeling behaviors that epitomize those core values? Have you rooted out all double standards? When certain employees are given a pass on values and held to a different standard, perhaps because of their position level or their specialized expertise and value to the organization, it creates a poisonous atmosphere that permeates the workforce. Even if everyone is politely withholding critical comments, that doesn't mean they don't sense it. It's the responsibility of senior leadership to clean up the environment. Don't tolerate double standards, nepotism, or cronyism. They are deadly enemies of trust in the workforce. Pay particular attention to inconsistencies regarding rewards. Nothing tends to erode trust more than pledging to reward one set of behaviors—quality, for instance— and then rewarding another, such as efficiency at the expense of quality. Pay attention to all messages and be disciplined to follow through consistently.

☐ **3. Make leadership intentions transparent.** If leaders feel compelled to obscure their intentions, something's amiss and will be reflected in loss of trust and disengagement of the workforce. Machiavellian duplicity might help win some battles but will lose the war. When hidden agendas come to light, trust in senior leadership takes a big hit. Better to come clean right away. Let employees know if there's a need to reduce the workforce, for instance. Let them know sooner rather than later. Tell them why. Ask them for help. Make decision-making processes as transparent and inclusive as possible. Of course, sometimes conditions and context restrict decisions to a small number of decision makers. Sometimes the buck stops at a single leader who must make a tough decision. If the decision is explained as quickly as possible after the fact—what the decision is, how it was made, why it had to be made within a certain time frame, why the number of decision makers was limited—such action is much more likely to be accepted and, in fact, likely to build trust rather than break it down. So make transparency the norm in your organization. Pull the wraps off your intentions.

☐ **4. Deal fairly but not equally.** Equal is not fair. Equal means the same treatment for everyone. Fair is what's appropriate, what's fitting. Individuals and teams vary in capabilities, motivation, interests, contribution, and many other dimensions. It follows then that, to be fair about it, they should be treated differently. Different levels of support. Different development. Different compensation. Different but fair. Compensating Jane at a higher level than Joe is fair if Jane's contribution to the organization exceeds Joe's. On the other hand, if Jane's slight padding of an expense account

33

is overlooked because she's a golfing buddy of a vice president but Joe is called on the same offense, that's not fair. It's a double standard, an inequity. And inequities of that type destroy trust. Preventing those kinds of problems depends on leadership that has the best of intentions for the organization and for individuals. As noted above, those intentions should be out in the open and clearly communicated. When one project team or business unit learns it's not getting the same level of resources that another is, it's tough to swallow if the intentions are concealed or suspect. On the other hand, the straightforward disclosure of intentions behind the decision makes it more acceptable. Even if the shortchanged team disagrees with the decision, they will appreciate understanding the intent behind it and trust in the leadership will be preserved, even strengthened.

☐ **5. Show compassion, especially in times of crisis.** All eyes turn to leaders in times of crisis. A steady resolve and stiff upper lip can help lead the workforce through tough times, but it's a good idea to also show sincere compassion for those who are enduring hardship. Visit those in distress. Listen to them. Offer them encouragement and whatever support possible. Care. Genuinely care. And let it show. Acknowledge fears and concerns and speak to what is being done to try to address them. Offer encouragement and, if possible, a helping hand to those who are striving hard but beginning to falter under the strain. Acknowledge those who have gone above and beyond the call of duty, those who have given extra effort and sacrifice to help achieve goals important to the organization. No one wants to see a leader tremble in the face of the same pressures everyone else is facing, but neither do they want to see someone who is aloof, detached, and unfeeling in difficult situations. Both approaches are unsettling and can undermine confidence and trust in leadership.

☐ **6. Put a personal face on leadership.** It can create real problems when leaders are tucked away in corner offices far removed from operations and rarely seen in person by the workforce. Isolated leaders will likely be viewed, at best, as detached, imperial, and indifferent to the needs of the workforce. In the worst case, many employees will be suspicious, resentful, and mistrusting of isolated leaders. Even if leaders' offices are located in the middle of the action, closed doors indicate isolation. Open the doors. Get out of the offices. Make personal contact so employees can see that leaders are real people. Ask questions. Lots of questions. Listen. Ask more. Listen more. Have meaningful conversations but don't dominate them. Get to know your people. Let down your guard so they get to know you. Don't have the time? Then what do you have time for? Stop making excuses. A simple, "Hey, what's up?" or "How did your meeting with Sam go?" can

B

34

start an important conversation. It shows interest. And personal contact turns senior leaders into "real people" and helps employees identify with them, to trust them, to want to follow them. Leaders need to break through the barriers, self-imposed or otherwise, and become more than "suits." Holding town hall meetings and flipping burgers at the company picnic is all fine and good, but that can easily be seen as window dressing. Go deeper. Do individuals know how executives got to where they are in the organization? What they did to succeed? The sacrifices they made? The hard lessons they learned? What they envision for the organization? What motivates them? What keeps them up at night? These are things that can be summarized in a company newsletter profile, but they are even more powerful when served up in personal conversations that take place in the work setting.

☐ **7. Engage in straight talk.** Sugarcoating bad news. Corporate-speak. Dancing around issues. All are signs of leadership weakness and serve to damage trust. Communicating in a straightforward, no-nonsense manner is a key leadership skill. Model it. Promote it. Don't tolerate prattling presentations dominated by slides that muddle the key issues. Call people on it. Direct them quickly to the heart of the matter. It's possible to be direct without screaming. To be blunt without being hurtful. Relentlessly develop EQ (Emotional Quotient) competencies in your leadership ranks. These are the competencies that enable effective interpersonal communication and cultivate meaningful relationships. Conflict management. Composure. Patience. Listening. Understanding others. These and other EQ competencies will enable effective straight talk that cuts through confusion, enhances leader credibility, and strengthens trust. Without EQ skills, straight talk can be an irrationally pounded hammer that does great damage.

☐ **8. Show some humility.** A paradox is an apparent contradiction. And effective leadership has more than a few. One striking paradox is the need for an effective leader to exude confidence as well as be willing to show humility, two seemingly contrary characteristics. Charismatic leaders, the leaders who give resounding stump speeches and carry a celebrity status, seem to get all the attention. But it's very often the more reserved leaders who deliver consistent results year in and year out. Charisma, personal magnetism, can lead to fervent devotion by followers. Not a bad thing unless it goes to the leader's head. In that case, the charismatic leader begins to swagger, becomes arrogant, assumes invincibility, and becomes the poster child for hubris. In such cases, trouble is not far off. Pride creates a psychological wall that suppresses approachability. Pride drowns out other voices so the ability to listen and receive input is squelched. Pride

35

stifles accountability. Confidence is something else altogether. Confidence comes from self-awareness, from thoroughly understanding strengths and weaknesses, from learning from experience, and from listening to others. Confidence and humility are not mutually exclusive. Embrace and promote both characteristics in your leadership ranks to engender trust and engagement.

☐ **9. Promote accountability, ownership, and personal responsibility.** Everyone in the organization has responsibility for delivering something of value. Everyone. But leaders bear the brunt of the responsibility for delivering results. They need to take personal responsibility when results fall short. The leader who takes personal responsibility steps up, delivers the news without making excuses, and candidly explains what went wrong. What went wrong should include a heavy dose of "I" statements. "I'm accountable for the project failing to meet its targets. I failed to monitor the project closely enough. I didn't recognize at an early stage when it was going off track. I didn't make sure the project team had sufficient resources. I take full responsibility. I own the problem, and here's what I'm doing to correct it...." Statements like those don't paint a picture of martyrdom. No one's a victim. But someone's responsible. Accountable. When things go right, when targets are met, that's the time to use "they" and "we" statements. "The project team did a superb job. We worked together early on to identify potential derailers, and the team raised an issue early on that we were able to resolve to keep the project on track. Here's what we learned from the project...." When leaders accept responsibility, when they demonstrate ownership, they build trust. They contribute to continuous improvement. They model the engagement behaviors that you want to develop in all employees. Promote those leaders. Weed out the others, those that shift blame and sidestep responsibility. There should be no room for them in your organization.

☐ **10. Share it all—the pain, pleasure, wealth, and knowledge.** True leaders are generous. They give of themselves for the greater good of the organization. They share. They serve. They sacrifice without wearing it on their sleeves. Their intentions can't be called into question, because their conduct is consistently above reproach. They model the behaviors that embody the core organizational values. Leaders are out in front and set the bar highest for themselves. They take risks and make sacrifices that can take many forms. Effort. Time. Money. Resources. Career security. Sacrifices should never be phony. But they should resonate with others. They don't have to be grand or dramatic, though there are certainly examples of a single act of sacrifice leaving such an impression that it defines a career. The CEO who foregoes pay until a business is turned around. The vice president who stands squarely in the media spotlight and takes the blame for a colossal service failure. The business unit head who works round the clock supporting three shifts in order to meet a critical customer need. Such notable sacrifices certainly give rise to loyalty, commitment, and engagement. But so do smaller deeds that might be less flashy but nonetheless meaningful to others. Sharing expertise. Coaching and mentoring. Teaching a business class. Volunteering in the community. There are a multitude of opportunities to share, to serve, to give. They make a difference.

> *Under pressure from Wall Street to maximize short-term earnings,*
> *boards of directors frequently chose leaders for their charisma*
> *instead of their character, their style rather than their substance,*
> *and their image instead of their integrity.*
> William W. George – Business professor, author,
> and former CEO of Medtronic

37

Suggested Readings

Albrecht, S., & Travaglione, A. (2003). Trust in public-sector senior management. *The International Journal of Human Resource Management, 14*, 76-92.

Bates, S. (2004). Getting engaged. *HR Magazine, 49*(2), 44-51.

Cawood, S., & Bailey, R. V. (2006). *Destination profit: Creating people-profit opportunities in your organization.* Mountain View, CA: Davies-Black.

Choi, Y., & Mai-Dalton, R. R. (1998). On the leadership function of self-sacrifice. *The Leadership Quarterly, 9*, 475-501.

Choi, Y., & Mai-Dalton, R. R. (1999). The model of followers' responses to self-sacrificial leadership: An empirical test. *The Leadership Quarterly, 10*, 397-421.

Fox, J. J. (2002). *How to become a great boss: The rules for getting and keeping the best employees.* NY: Hyperion.

George, B. (2007). *True north: Discover your authentic leadership.* San Francisco: Jossey-Bass.

Gillespie, N. A., & Mann, L. (2004). Transformational leadership and shared values: The building blocks of trust. *Journal of Managerial Psychology, 19*, 588-607.

Greenberg, J. (1986). Determinants of perceived fairness of performance evaluations. *Journal of Applied Psychology, 71*, 340-342.

Harvey, E. L., & Lucia, A. D. (1995). *Walk the talk: And get the results you want.* Dallas, TX: Performance Publishing.

Harvey, E. L., & Lucia, A. D. (1997). *144 Ways to walk the talk.* Dallas, TX: Performance Systems Corp.

Kim, W. C., & Mauborgne, R. (2003). Fair process: Managing in the knowledge economy. *Harvard Business Review, 81*(1), 127-136.

Kouzes, J. M., & Posner, B. Z. (2003). *The five practices of exemplary leadership.* San Francisco: John Wiley & Sons.

Mayer, R. C., Davis, J. H., & Schoorman, D. F. (1995). An integrative model of organizational trust. *Academy of Management Review, 20*, 709-734.

McShane, S. L., & Von Glinow, M. A. (2008). *Organizational behavior: Emerging realities for the workplace revolution* (4th ed.). NY: McGraw-Hill/Irwin.

Morgan, D. E., & Zeffane, R. (2003). Employee involvement, organizational change, and trust in management. *International Journal of Human Resource Management, 14*, 55-75.

Podsakoff, P. M., Mackenzie, S. B., Moorman, R. H., & Fetter, R. (1990). Transformational leader behaviors and their effects on followers' trust in leader, satisfaction, and organizational citizenship behaviors. *The Leadership Quarterly, 1*, 107-142.

Reichheld, F. F. (2001). Lead for loyalty. *Harvard Business Review, 79*(7), 76-84.

Robinson, S. L. (1996). Trust and breach of the psychological contract. *Administrative Science Quarterly, 41*, 574-599.

van Knippenberg, B., & van Knippenberg, D. (2005). Leader self-sacrifice and leadership effectiveness: The moderating role of leader prototypicality. *Journal of Applied Psychology, 90*, 25-37.

B

Engagement Driver C
Immediate Manager Working Relationship

The task of the leader is to get his people
from where they are to where they have not been.
Henry Kissinger – Former U.S. Secretary of State

The Signpost
The relationship between an employee and the immediate manager is one of the most powerful engagement drivers. It's widely recognized that while people join organizations for a variety of reasons, people frequently leave because of a poor relationship with their boss. It follows, then, that a primary way to enhance retention and engagement of your workforce is to make sure your management ranks are staffed with solid, effective leaders.

Unskilled
- ☐ Selects managers for technical skills rather than people management skills
- ☐ Fails to collaborate and clearly establish goals and expectations
- ☐ Doesn't provide adequate or effective performance feedback and coaching
- ☐ Inaccurately assesses talent; doesn't differentiate talent effectively
- ☐ Fails to provide managers with necessary training and resources
- ☐ Lacks ability to effectively provide coaching and resources for career development
- ☐ Tolerates mediocrity in the management ranks; allows marginal performers to slide
- ☐ Overwhelms management with unreasonable workload
- ☐ Doesn't have a safe process for employees to raise issues and concerns
- ☐ Fails to hold managers accountable for engaging their employees
- ☐ Fosters a culture of mistrust, intolerance, and suspicion
- ☐ Allows employee relation problems to fester; slow to respond

Skilled
- ☐ Makes frequent, meaningful conversations the centerpiece of the manager-employee relationship
- ☐ Fosters a culture of mutual respect, tolerance, openness, and trust
- ☐ Has a rigorous management selection process
- ☐ Assesses management performance frequently; takes action based on the results

- ☐ Effectively develops current and future managers to address skill gaps
- ☐ Infuses the work environment with feedback and coaching
- ☐ Provides managers with the skills and resources they need to provide career guidance
- ☐ Establishes an effective performance management process
- ☐ Retains, rewards, and promotes the best managers; moves bad managers out
- ☐ Provides a line of sight for managers to engagement results; holds them accountable
- ☐ Solicits input from employees; provides means for employees to raise issues and voice concerns without fear of reprisal
- ☐ Implements systems, organizational structure, and policies that empower managers and support best management practices

Some Causes

- ☐ Complacency; tolerance for mediocrity
- ☐ Dysfunctional reward system; good management not adequately rewarded
- ☐ Inappropriate organizational structure; spans of control too large
- ☐ Ineffective selection processes
- ☐ Insufficient management development resources
- ☐ Intolerant of diversity
- ☐ Conflict avoidance
- ☐ Inattention to career development
- ☐ Inadequate support systems for management
- ☐ Unsophisticated performance metrics and assessment methods

The Ten Leadership Architect® Competencies Most Associated with This Engagement Driver *(in order of connectedness)*

33. Listening
12. Conflict Management
56. Sizing Up People
13. Confronting Direct Reports
29. Integrity and Trust
36. Motivating Others
41. Patience
 3. Approachability
11. Composure
19. Developing Direct Reports and Others

The Map

The employee-manager relationship. Research indicates it's the single most important lever to drive engagement and retention. If you can only focus and work on one engagement driver, choose this one. Nothing else has the same impact. Career opportunities, nature of the job, recognition, pay, and other drivers are all important. But the relationship between the employee and immediate manager is, in general, more important than any other driver. People join good companies. People leave bad managers. Studies bear this out. The employee-manager relationship is the single biggest factor affecting employee satisfaction. And conflict with the immediate manager is a frequently cited factor in exit interviews as contributing to the decision to leave an organization. So develop a good employment brand to attract top talent. And develop an outstanding management cadre to keep top talent. Of the two, it takes longer and is generally more difficult to develop an outstanding employment brand. In fact, it's somewhat out of your control because your employment brand will largely be defined by your industry segment and financial performance. Is your business in a sexy, high-growth industry segment? Does your business have a successful long-term financial track record? How about short-term growth rate that looks like a rocket trajectory? Any of these factors simplify employment branding. You'll be much more likely to have A-list talent lining up for open positions. On the other hand, businesses in slow-growth markets and dull, unappealing industries have a tough challenge to attract top talent. In either case, recruitment is likely to be one of the top HR initiatives and requires significant effort and resources. Don't make the mistake of slighting management development at the expense of employment branding and recruitment. The quality of your management team directly impacts the performance and retention of your existing workforce. Bad managers debilitate performance and drive away good employees. Good managers get the most out of their employees. They create stickiness in the organization because top performers don't want to leave high-performance organizations. Good managers create winning teams. And winning builds your employment brand. There's no chicken-and-egg question here. Good management comes first. Develop your managers to make it easier to develop your employment brand. Good managers, of course, are competent in basic management skills: organizing, planning, directing others, time management, delegation, priority setting, informing, developing people, etc. But they also shine in personal and interpersonal skills. They are good listeners. They are approachable and fair. They manage conflict. Good management is a key to engaging talent. Make management development a top priority.

Some Remedies

☐ **1. Hire and promote the best managers.** It's a big leap to go from individual contributor to a first-line manager. The skills that help a person excel as an individual contributor—things such as technical proficiency and action orientation—aren't skills that help much when managing others. Good people managers have strong interpersonal skills. They know how to develop people and have a knack for getting work done through others rather than doing it themselves. Research clearly indicates that a lack of core interpersonal skills is a primary contributor to derailment in managers who fail. Look for these interpersonal skills when hiring and promoting people into management positions. Use behavioral interviewing techniques to check for people-related competencies. Sizing up others. Motivating others. Caring about people. Approachability. Listening. Patience. Composure. Fairness. Developing others. Elicit concrete examples that demonstrate a history of growth and development and success in applying these competencies. How have they successfully motivated others? In what way do they actively listen? What are their success stories around developing others? How have they failed? What did they learn from their failures? Check for self-awareness. Do they learn from experience? Do they avoid repeating mistakes? The self-aware candidate is a better bet for development. They seek feedback, gain insights from mistakes, and grow as a result. Design a rigorous selection process to ensure you get the right people in the key management positions that will impact performance and engagement.

☐ **2. Make management development a priority.** It's not enough to select the best management candidates; you need to help them continuously grow and learn. Managers do the heavy lifting when it comes to engaging employees, and the organization demonstrates that engagement is a priority when it provides training and development on the skills that drive engagement. Devote at least as much energy to training people management skills as to training technical skills. Structure curricula around people management skills, like coaching and giving feedback. Studies show that training supervisors to give positive and constructive feedback improves employee job satisfaction and performance. The best managers are expert coaches. They have finely tuned listening skills. They have meaningful conversations that help employees understand what needs to be accomplished and how behaviors impact others. In those conversations, they are present and focused on the employee. Not checking e-mail. Not glancing at their watch. They connect because they're truly interested and want the best for the employee and the organization. They raise self-awareness in others. They coach them in how to improve performance. They resolve conflicts, address them constructively and head-on. They ask questions that encourage involvement. They promote a sense of ownership. They motivate, get others fired up about meeting team goals. All these management behaviors drive engagement and organizational performance. Such skills should be taught and practiced in your management development programs. Incorporate role-plays and simulations so managers practice coaching, practice having difficult conversations, and get lots of feedback from their peers.

☐ **3. Make collaborative goal setting the norm.** Research shows that highly engaged employees are goal oriented. And disengaged employees are often unclear about what's expected of them. Shared goals benefit the organization because they get everyone on the same page and pulling in the same direction. Efforts are coordinated and aligned. Goals provide clarity of purpose. Focus. They provide the basis for assessment of performance and enable more effective coaching. When managers collaborate with their employees to establish goals, they increase buy-in and motivation. Personal communication around goals fosters ownership and understanding. It's an opportunity to help employees see how their accomplishments make a difference and fit in the big picture. When employees have a sense of personal accountability for achieving goals, engagement increases. Urge managers to collaborate with employees in one-on-one meetings to define, review, and revise goals. Generally, people perform better with goals that can be realistically reached by putting forth significant effort. Stretch goals are especially helpful in pushing for new skills. Research shows that when goals are set appropriately and communicated clearly, engagement increases.

☐ **4. Provide tools, systems, and policies to support managers.** Managers have a lot on their plates. They are constantly juggling multiple roles. As agents of the organization, managers interpret policies and influence how they are applied to employees. As bosses, they are pivotal partners in the contract that affects employees' commitment to the job. And don't forget the constant pressure to "make the numbers." In the midst of all the tasks to be done, managers have to make time for employees. They have to make time to have personal interaction, to coach, to have conversations. When meetings, phone calls, e-mail, and paperwork consume ten hours in a typical day, the manager is in a no-win situation. Making time for personal interaction is futile. It's unfair to managers and employees alike. Do what needs to be done to give managers more time. Reduce paperwork. Limit meetings. Implement systems that reduce the administrative burden. Design the organization so there are reasonable spans of control. Revamp policies and procedures that put unnecessary burden on management. We

43

need laws because some people don't act responsibly. We need a police force because some people disobey the laws. How much would go away if everyone was responsible? So it goes in an organization. When you have engaged, competent, and responsible employees, policies and procedures can be minimized. Managers don't have to be cops. Measurement and control will always be part of management. But measurement and control shouldn't be all-consuming. Examine all policies and procedures and consider the cost in terms of management time required. Prune out the bureaucracy and administrivia to free up managers' time to do what they should be doing—focusing on people.

☐ **5. Build a feedback-rich environment.** At the outset of the supervisor-employee relationship, establish a high-candor-feedback protocol. Managers should explain that the purpose of feedback is to help guide and support the employee to be successful in the job. In addition to setting the expectation that the employee will regularly receive candid feedback, the manager should also ask for regular feedback from the employee. Establishing expectations around feedback in this way communicates positive intent and helps remove tension. In organizations that have created a culture steeped in candor and straight talk, giving and receiving feedback is as natural as breathing. Feedback is given frequently, usually in real time during and immediately following performance. The feedback is tied to goals. Performance goals. Developmental goals. Career goals. Feedback on performance helps employees adjust what they are doing along the way and make midcourse corrections. Developmental and career feedback shows employees that what they are doing is important and that the manager is there to help them grow and progress with the organization. Encourage managers to view giving—and receiving—feedback as a gift, not a burden. Start a campaign. Begin at the top. A campaign to give more candid and critical feedback. Require performance evaluation grades to be distributed or rank ordered. Require managers to spread out their ratings. Make sure feedback is balanced with as much critical and constructive feedback as positive. Use 360° techniques. Anonymous feedback tends to be more accurate than face-to-face. Make your environment a feedback-rich environment, and supplement the feedback with coaching and mentoring to encourage and guide development in the core competencies.

☐ **6. Put teeth into engagement.** Conduct periodic surveys to assess engagement levels in the organization, and give managers a clear line of sight to the survey results. Slice the data so individual managers can see results for which they are accountable. From senior leadership down to first-line management, find ways to link engagement results to tangible consequences. If the organization uses a balanced scorecard, incorporate engagement metrics. Set engagement goals and communicate them throughout the organization. Track retention in each manager's area as another measure of engagement. Publicly celebrate those managers and teams who exemplify high engagement. Likewise, a manager who hits other productivity targets should not be immune from adverse consequences when engagement is low. Allot a percentage of manager incentive compensation to engagement results.

☐ **7. Put a focus on career development.** Employees want to see a career path, to know about development opportunities, to understand career options that are available in the organization. And they look first to their boss for guidance. Prepare your managers to provide that guidance. Communicate the availability of development opportunities to managers so they can pass them along as appropriate. Encourage managers to participate in workforce planning so they understand the forecasted employment landscape. So they know where skill gaps currently exist. Where they are likely to exist in the future. Involve managers in succession planning meetings. Teach them to assess talent, to differentiate performance and potential, to talk talent. Design and implement a formal career development process in the organization and devote resources to it. Give managers the information and tools they need to explain how careers are developed in the organization, how the career paths evolve for professionals and general managers, and how to best prepare to successfully navigate a chosen path.

☐ **8. Embrace diversity of all types.** Employees feel valued when their opinions are valued. Managers who encourage different points of view and are receptive to input from all employees have more productive and satisfying working relationships. And organizations that nurture diversity of opinions and ideas have a competitive advantage over those that don't. Create a common mind-set around diversity. Take a broad view to include diversity of thought and ideas. Foster a culture of inclusion and openness. Consider different answers, reasons, or approaches to problems—think differently. Challenge traditional views and perspectives—don't suppress unconventional thinking. Take a new look at vexing problems from diverse viewpoints. Turn off internal judgment programs. Ask open-ended questions that encourage new viewpoints. What would you change? How do you feel about that? Managers who respect varying opinions and viewpoints make a positive impact on engagement.

☐ **9. Provide a safe harbor for employees.** Sometimes the boss-subordinate relationship gets damaged. An employee may feel it's not possible to work through an issue with the manager for any number of reasons. They may feel that they won't be heard. That they won't be understood. That they

45

will face retribution. For whatever reason the employee perceives, there should be a way to vent concerns about individual managers. Design feedback mechanisms that do or don't protect anonymity, depending on the organization culture. Conduct periodic surveys so employees can air concerns. This is also a great way for HR and management to gather data on employee engagement levels. Suggestion boxes or Web sites send a message to employees that their viewpoint matters. Plan skip-level meetings to give employees a chance to talk to the boss's boss about what's on their minds. Establish an ombudsman process. In non-union shops, ombudsmen offer neutral, informal, confidential help for employees who want their problems addressed but not advertised. Make sure employees can see that their opinions matter and that the organization will take action based on their concerns. Conduct exit interviews with employees who leave. Make sure bad bosses are not causing unwanted turnover.

☐ **10. Remove managers who don't make the grade.** Assess manager performance regularly and include measures of people management—employee engagement and retention—in addition to the typical financial and productivity metrics. When a manager is having a negative impact on the workforce, have the courage to act quickly. Put the manager on notice. Have the tough conversation. Give them candid, timely, and actionable feedback. Put them on a short improvement plan. Provide all of the help that is practical. Closely monitor their progress. If there isn't a meaningful change, take decisive action. Institutionalize the practice of releasing marginal performers. Learn how to spot bad boss behaviors in the organization. Beware the manager who is surrounded with cronies that parrot the same views and don't step out of line. Does the manager rake people over the coals in public? Make others feel stupid? Verbally abuse? In the Center for Creative Leadership's research, successful senior executives reported that working for a bad boss provided rich learning in their careers. They learned what *not* to do, how *not* to act. But you can't afford to keep bad managers around as examples of what not to do. The risk is that they will drive away good employees. And consider this: When employees leave the organization because of a bad boss, who ends up doing the replacement hiring? In one organization, 80% of new employees were being hired by the bottom 40% of their managers. Avoid this vicious cycle by ferreting out bad bosses. Either develop their interpersonal and people management skills or show them the door.

> *There are managers so preoccupied with their e-mail messages*
> *that they never look up from their screens*
> *to see what's happening in the non-digital world.*
> Mihaly Csikszentmihalyi – Author and Professor of Psychology

Suggested Readings

Bates, S. (2004). Getting engaged. *HR Magazine, 49*(2), 44-51.

Branham, F. L. (2001). *Keeping the people who keep you in business: 24 Ways to hang on to your most valuable talent.* NY: AMACOM.

Brousseau, K. R., Driver, M. J., Hourihan, G., & Larsson, R. (2006). The seasoned executive's decision-making style. *Harvard Business Review, 84*(2), 110-121.

Cawood, S., & Bailey, R. V. (2006). *Destination profit: Creating people-profit opportunities in your organization.* Mountain View, CA: Davies-Black.

Dai, G., Tang, K. Y., & De Meuse, K. P. (2008, April). *Leadership competencies across position levels: Test of the pipeline model.* Research paper presented at the Society for Industrial and Organizational Psychology Conference, San Francisco.

Dixon-Kheir, C. (2001). Supervisors are key to keeping young talent. *HR Magazine, 46*(1), 139-142.

Eichinger, R. W., Lombardo, M. M., & Ulrich, D. (2004). *100 Things you need to know: Best people practices for managers & HR.* Minneapolis, MN: Lominger International: A Korn/Ferry Company.

Fox, J. J. (2002). *How to become a great boss: The rules for getting and keeping the best employees.* NY: Hyperion.

Gabarro, J. (1979). Socialization at the top: How CEOs and subordinates evolve interpersonal contracts. *Organizational Dynamics, 7*(3), 2-23.

Hirschman, C., Mirza, P., & Shea, T. F. (2003). Someone to listen. *HR Magazine, 48*(1), 46-52.

Hornstein, H. A. (1996). *Brutal bosses and their prey: How to identify and overcome abuse in the workplace.* NY: Riverhead Books.

Johnson, H. (2001). Knowing your employee. *Training, 38*(10), 30.

Joinson, C. (2001). Employee sculpt thyself...with a little help. *HR Magazine, 46*(5), 60-65.

Kouzes, J. M., & Posner, B. Z. (2003). *Encouraging the heart: A leader's guide to rewarding and recognizing others.* San Francisco: Jossey-Bass.

McCall, M., Lombardo, M. M., & Morrison A. (1988). *The lessons of experience: How successful executives develop on the job.* NY: Free Press.

Neves, P., & Caetano, A. (2006). Social exchange processes in organizational change: The roles of trust and control. *Journal of Change Management, 6*, 351-364.

Rosas-Gaddi, R. C. (2006). *Leadership and employee engagement: When employees give their all.* Retrieved January 15, 2009, from http://www.ddiworld.com/htm/ddi_ph_leadershipandemployeeengagement_ar.htm

Smith, B., & Rutigliano, T. (2002). The truth about turnover. *Gallup Management Journal Online*, 1-5.

Towers Perrin. (2005). *Winning strategies for a global workforce: Attracting, retaining, and engaging employees for competitive advantage.* Retrieved January 15, 2009, from http://www.towersperrin.com/tp/getwebcachedoc?webc=HRS/USA/2006/200602/GWS.pdf

Ulrich, D., Eichinger, R. W., Kulas, J. T., & De Meuse, K. P. (2007). *50 More things you need to know: The science behind best people practices for managers & HR professionals.* Minneapolis, MN: Lominger International: A Korn/Ferry Company.

Whitworth, B., & Riccomini, B. (2005). Unlocking higher employee performance. *Communication World, 22*(2), 18-22.

Zenger, J., & Folkman, J. (2002). *The extraordinary leader: Turning good managers into great leaders.* NY: McGraw-Hill.

Engagement Driver D
Peer Culture

The Signpost

If there is dysfunction in your organization's peer networks, your employees will dread going to work just as a person would dread going to the reunion of a dysfunctional family. When your organization's peer networks are well-oiled and effective, the opposite will be true. Employees will look forward to going to work just as a person from a loving family looks forward to seeing siblings and long-lost cousins. It's all about relationships, and the culture you foster in your organization will promote effective relationships, or not. Effective peer relationships lead to highly engaged, productive employees.

Unskilled

- ☐ Allows organizational roadblocks and physical obstacles to peer interaction
- ☐ Generally restricts personal interactions with peers to compulsory meetings
- ☐ Tolerates turf battles and low levels of cooperation between peers
- ☐ Allows criticism and backbiting to pervade the workplace
- ☐ Fails to establish opportunity for frequent social interaction between peers
- ☐ Permits a climate that is exclusionary and unwelcoming to newcomers
- ☐ Communicates ineffectively and not in a timely manner
- ☐ Fails to extend the onboarding process to internal transfers
- ☐ Makes staffing decisions with little or no input from peer network
- ☐ Neglects knowledge-sharing processes and technology

Skilled

- ☐ Promotes peer coaching and mentoring networks
- ☐ Plans and organizes opportunities for peer social interaction
- ☐ Fosters a culture of trust, respect, and openness
- ☐ Develops conflict-management skills at all levels in the organization

☐ Establishes communication processes and channels to enhance information sharing between workgroups

☐ Designs workspaces that encourage personal interaction

☐ Recognizes and rewards peer collaboration

☐ Creates an effective onboarding process that addresses internal transfers as well as new hires

☐ Identifies and reduces organizational silos and other barriers to cooperation

☐ Implements knowledge-sharing processes and technology that enable peers to easily connect and share expertise

Some Causes

☐ Dysfunctional internal competition; competing goals

☐ Leader defensiveness

☐ Limited resources

☐ Poor time management

☐ Silo mentality; personal fiefdoms

☐ Insufficient rewards for team performance and collaboration

☐ Inadequate communication skills

☐ Suspicion; lack of trust

☐ Prevalence of counterproductive internal politics

☐ Ineffective staffing practices

The Ten Leadership Architect® Competencies Most Associated with This Engagement Driver (in order of connectedness)

42. Peer Relationships
60. *Building Effective* Teams
12. Conflict Management
33. Listening
38. Organizational Agility
46. Perspective
25. Hiring and Staffing
29. Integrity and Trust
31. Interpersonal Savvy
56. Sizing Up People

The Map

Peers, by definition, have some things in common. They probably share one or more important characteristics related to status in the organization: position level, scope of responsibility, and budgetary authority, for example.

Peers also likely share personal attributes—key skills and abilities, educational attainment, career goals, motivation, even demographic traits. So it's likely that no one in the workplace understands you quite like a peer. At their best, peer relationships provide emotional support, spur professional growth, impart cultural and political knowledge, encourage collaboration and innovation, and extend personal influence. Yet in many organizations, the benefits of peer relationships are overlooked and development of peer networks is left to chance. In those firms, highly productive peer relationships exist, if they exist at all, in spite of the organization. It's a bad idea to leave peer relationships to chance. When dysfunctional, they create noise in the organization. They stir up undercurrents that distract people from what's important. Constrict the sharing of information. Cause resources to be hoarded. Undermine engagement. Damage trust. Drive fun out of the business. And all because the organization doesn't get it, doesn't understand the importance of promoting peer relationships. But some organizations do get it. They don't leave things to chance. They understand that productive peer relationships increase engagement and drive organizational performance. So they actively promote networking, collaboration, and communities of practice. They commit time and resources to building relationships. They don't allow peer conflicts to simmer, hoping they'll somehow magically disappear. Instead, they address conflict early and directly. They pay attention to the details of relationships and take action when it's required. Good things happen in those firms as peers develop personal relationships and trust in each other. Those relationships reduce friction in the organization. The gears of organizational change get lubricated. Work gets done faster. People look out for each other. Mistakes decrease. Quality and customer service improve. Information is shared more freely. Feedback is provided more freely and candidly. Resources are used more efficiently. Business becomes fun, engaging.

Some Remedies

☐ **1. Help people to personally connect.** Communication technology is great for saving time and travel costs, but there is no substitute for personal interaction. Make sure that peer groups have opportunities for up-close and personal interaction. They need to rub shoulders. To really get to know each other. And not just in business meetings. Plan events that bring peers together to socialize in addition to conducting business. Create, support, and facilitate professional groups, local chapters of national organizations, volunteer groups, hobby groups, after-work sports teams. All of these provide opportunities for peers to connect in different ways. Put special focus on the activities of peer groups that are critically important to the organization. Use the training function to build peer relationships by strategically populating training events. At times, the objectives of training are best served by including heterogeneous groups that span multiple levels in the organization, especially when the training is part of an organizational change effort. But some programs are ideal for bringing peers together. Leadership development, for instance, generally spans business functions but targets a particular management level. A peer cohort will benefit from the relationships formed through interaction in such programs. Spend the time and effort to get the right mix of peers in the program. Bring people together who rarely have an opportunity to interact because they're from disparate functions, business units, or geographical regions. The point is to be deliberate, to build peer relationships strategically rather than to invite participants solely based on scheduling convenience.

☐ **2. Design workspaces to optimize interaction.** Every physical structure has inherent limitations that will restrict what can be done with the design of workspaces. Look for ways to work within the limitations of your facilities to optimize productive work relationships. Research shows that there is a definite correlation between the physical distance separating people and the frequency of their communication. Simply, when people are separated by a distance of 50 meters or more, there is less communication. Peers who are co-located will communicate more frequently. In addition to analyzing physical distance, consider how to design workspace to accommodate incidental, unplanned interactions. Include sufficient meeting space to handle groups of various sizes for private work sessions. To the extent possible, provide visual access to the surrounding workplace so people are aware of activity and the movement of others and can see opportunities to interact. Strike a balance between providing necessary privacy and opening up the workplace to encourage collaboration and face-to-face communication.

☐ **3. Remove organizational barriers to transfers.** Physical boundaries imposed by facilities are sometimes easier to remove than self-imposed organizational boundaries. They shouldn't be. Be relentless in identifying protected turf, sacred cows, and narrow-minded and selfish leaders who build walls around their talent for fear of losing key personnel. Tear down those walls. Strategically assign people to jobs to cross-pollinate the organization and provide key exposures. Plan for some percentage of inter-unit job transfers to occur in every business cycle. Make it an expectation. Reward leaders who develop their people and free them to move to other parts of the business. Learning from a diverse array of jobs is the primary way in which leadership skills are developed. Variety in job assignments also provides opportunities to build peer relationships that enhance people skills, extend personal influence, and develop organizational savvy. Master the science of strategically deploying talent to jobs for development. When you do, you'll be helping peer networks to develop.

☐ **4. Build relationships through short-term assignments.** There's a practical limit to the number of job transfers that an organization can digest. Cross-functional project teams, task forces, and other special assignments provide an alternate way to build peer relationships. When handpicked members from finance, engineering, marketing, and logistics get together to work on an important issue, great things can happen. In addition to the creative solutions that are often generated by the different perspectives, new relationships are formed. Team members get a greater understanding and appreciation of different parts of the organization. They learn how their individual and departmental performance affects others in the organization. Cross-functional teams and task forces are high-impact developmental experiences. Members are forced to govern themselves, deal with ambiguous circumstances, plan, negotiate, navigate organizational politics, and sell their combined vision to the rest of the organization. In peer groups, the ability to influence without authority becomes critical. All of the skills learned can be transferred to other job situations in the future. All these benefits make a strong case for uniting peers across the organization to solve enterprise-wide problems.

☐ **5. Recognize and reward team efforts and collaboration.** Most recognition and reward systems are designed to reinforce the performance of the individual. Most significant business results, though, are achieved through the collaborative efforts of many individuals and groups. Those collaborative efforts should receive ample recognition. Find success stories of teamwork and collaboration and communicate them consistently. Implement a system for collecting and sharing details about organizational citizenship behaviors (OCBs)—selfless acts of individuals and teams that serve the larger good. Promote people into leadership who demonstrate the willingness and capacity for team building. It's probably not enough to tout the value of teamwork but then only reward individual contribution. Consider how to reward teams in addition to rewarding individuals. Use care to ensure you're not creating internal competition in which one individual or team wins by making another individual or team in the organization lose.

☐ **6. Support communities of practice.** Provide resources for groups with common interests to share knowledge, develop best practices, and advance their expertise. Create and publish directories of experts. Provide behind-the-firewall technologies—social networking, blogs, wikis, social filtering, online communities, tagging and social bookmarking—whatever will best facilitate collaboration and learning. Study how the military is using communities of practice (CoPs) to promote rapid organizational learning in unstable and unforgiving environments. Consider how to sanction and support Skunk Works project teams.

☐ **7. Teach conflict-management skills.** Conflicts happen. Peers sometimes clash. Disputes over resources. Incompatible personalities. Philosophical differences. Regardless of the cause, conflicts provide an opportunity to build relationships and learn. Conflict-management skills are among the most critical and difficult competencies to develop. Since opportunities for conflict occur so frequently, the organization can serve as an ongoing classroom to teach key principles of conflict management. When addressing conflict, encourage individuals to think in shades of gray rather than rigid black-and-white terms. Reflect on the perspectives and values that are at the root of conflict. Acknowledge differing viewpoints. Deal with emotions. Refrain from playing the part of referee or parent and declaring a winner. Instead, listen. Calm things down. Perhaps offer just a few thoughts to consider and then allow the parties to work it out away from your watchful eye. After things have cooled off and, hopefully, been resolved, ask for an update about how the issue was resolved and what was learned from the experience. This provides accountability and ensures that action will be taken instead of following the urge to avoid the conflict. Eventually, participants will develop their skills and bring their own hard-fought wisdom to future conflicts. And don't forget, the senior leadership peer group is modeling peer conflict management for the rest of the organization.

☐ **8. Support peer-to-peer coaching networks.** Research supports positive outcomes from peer mentoring relationships, including buffers from stress, higher job satisfaction, and lower turnover. Peers can form more effective bonds when they are actively helping each other perform, learn, grow, and advance. This is a different type of mentoring relationship than the traditional under-the-wing partnership between a higher-ranking, more tenured employee and an up-and-comer. The arrangement is less formal and the dialogue between participants may be freer and more open on political matters. The idea is to have a private insider to turn to for coaching and advice. Someone who can help the person being mentored to learn the ropes and make contact with key influencers. New employee onboarding is a great opportunity to establish a peer-to-peer coaching relationship. Provide training, tools, and support for coaches and mentors. Be a matchmaker. Help peers connect. Then step aside and allow the relationship to naturally evolve.

☐ **9. Build peer collaboration into hiring processes.** Involve peers in interviewing and hiring decisions to promote cooperation and deepen understanding of the needs of other work units. Peers can provide a valuable perspective and can contribute to sizing up a candidate's cultural fit with the organization. It's good for the candidate, too, to get insight into the broader organization during the interview process and hear how the immediate workgroup is perceived by one or more of the hiring manager's peers. Candidates may feel freer to pose tough questions to a peer than to the prospective immediate boss or an HR representative and more likely to receive realistic insight into daily life in the organization in the process. Ideally, all interviewers, including peers, provide input for consideration to the hiring manager. Ultimately, the hiring manager is accountable for the decision but should consider and express appreciation for all input and then provide some rationale for the final decision.

☐ **10. Encourage peers to frequently share work-related information.** Sometimes all it takes to get peers collaborating is to let them know what others are up to. On cross-functional projects, periodically invite key stakeholders to informational meetings. Report out on progress. Issues to be resolved. Lessons learned. Just by being included, peers from other groups will be better connected to what's going on and broaden their perspectives and understanding of how things come together in the bigger picture. Disagreements over deliverables, schedules, resources, and other issues will be resolved more effectively when people are adequately informed. Occasionally invite peers who are not directly involved in a project to informational meetings. Solicit their perspectives, ideas, and solutions. Including peers in meetings to share information maintains and reinforces goal alignment. It's important to ensure that business unit and department goals are not only aligned with top-level business objectives, but that they complement the goals of other workgroups. Staying informed means staying aligned.

Meanwhile, the originator of a theory may have a very lonely time,
especially if his colleagues find his views of nature unfamiliar,
and difficult to appreciate.
Peter D. Mitchell – British biochemist and Nobel Prize winner

Suggested Readings

Allen, T. D., Russell, J. A., & Maetzke, S. B. (1997). Formal peer mentoring: Factors related to protégés' satisfaction and willingness to mentor others. *Group & Organization Management, 22*, 488-507.

Bennett, E. (2008). *Social software's culture clash*. Retrieved January 15, 2009, from http://www.baselinemag.com/c/a/Messaging-and-Collaboration/Social-Softwares-Culture-Clash/

Cohen, D., & Prusak, L. (2001). *In good company: How social capital makes organizations work.* Boston, MA: Harvard Business School Press.

Daniels, A. C. (2000). *Bringing out the best in people: How to apply the astonishing power of positive reinforcement.* NY: McGraw-Hill.

Decktop, J. R., Mangel, R., & Cirka, C. C. (1999). Getting more than you pay for: Organizational citizenship behavior and pay-for-performance plans. *Academy of Management Journal, 42,* 420–428.

Hildreth, P., & Kimble, C. (2004). *Knowledge networks: Innovation through communities of practice.* London: Hershey Idea Group.

Johnson, J. (2004, May). *The knowledge workplace: Designing for interaction.* Retrieved January 15, 2009, from http://www.isdesignet.com/articles/detail.aspx?contentID=4685

Kram, K. E., & Isabella, L. A. (1985). Mentoring alternatives: The role of peer relationships in career development. *Academy of Management Journal, 28,* 110-132.

Liu, C. M., Chien, C. W., Chou, P., Liu, J. H., Chen, V. T., Wei, J., Kuo, Y. Y., & Lang, H. C. (2005). An analysis of job satisfaction among physician assistants in Taiwan. *Health Policy, 73,* 66-77.

McShane, S. L., & Von Glinow, M. A. (2008). *Organizational behavior: Emerging realities for the workplace revolution* (4th ed.). NY: McGraw-Hill/Irwin.

Modaff, D. P., & DeWine, S. (2002). *Organizational communication: Foundations, challenges, and misunderstandings.* Los Angeles: Roxbury. Retrieved January 15, 2009, from D. R. Lane (2002), Professor, University of Kentucky, Communication Department Web site: www.uky.edu/~drlane/orgcomm/325ch11.ppt

Morrison, E. W. (2002). Newcomers' relationships: The role of social network ties during socialization. *Academy of Management Journal, 45,* 1149-1160.

Park, K. O., & Wilson, M. G. (2003). Psychosocial work environments and psychological strain among Korean factory workers. *Stress & Health, 19,* 173-179.

Raabe, B., & Beehr, T. A. (2003). Formal mentoring versus supervisor and coworker relationships: Differences in perceptions and impact. *Journal of Organizational Behavior, 24,* 271-293.

Saint-Onge, H., & Wallace, D. (2003). *Leveraging communities of practice for strategic advantage.* Boston, MA: Butterworth-Heinemann.

Siegel, P. H., Reinstein, A., Karim, K. E., & Rigsby, J. T. (1998). The role of peer relationships during CPA firm mergers. *Behavioral Research in Accounting, 10,* 270-277.

Sirota, D., Mischkind, L. A., & Meltzer, M. I. (2005). *The enthusiastic employee: How companies profit by giving workers what they want.* Upper Saddle River, NJ: Wharton School Publishing.

Towers Perrin. (2003). *The 2003 Towers Perrin Talent Report: Working today: Understanding what drives employee engagement.* Retrieved January 15, 2009, from http://www.towersperrin.com/tp/getwebcachedoc?webc=HRS/USA/2003/200309/Talent_2003.pdf

Tracy, B. (2004). Top five reasons people stay in their jobs. *CPA Journal, 74*, 17.

Tsai, P. C., Yen, Y. F., Huang, L. C., & Huang, I. C. (2007). A study on motivating employees' learning commitment in the post-downsizing era: Job satisfaction perspective. *Journal of World Business, 42*, 157-169.

Ulrich, D., Eichinger, R. W., Kulas, J. T., & De Meuse, K. P. (2007). *50 More things you need to know: The science behind best people practices for managers & HR professionals*. Minneapolis, MN: Lominger International: A Korn/Ferry Company.

Wenger, E., McDermott, R., & Snyder, W. M. (2002). *Cultivating communities of practice: A guide to managing knowledge*. Boston, MA: Harvard Business School Press.

Whitney, K. (2007a). Reasons for failed mentor programs might be rooted in psychology. *Chief Learning Officer*. Retrieved January 15, 2009, from http://tinyurl.com/2mkz22

Whitney, K. (2007b). U.S. Army: Sharing lessons from the field. *Chief Learning Officer*. Retrieved January 15, 2009, from http://www.clomedia.com/in-practice/2007/October/1959/index.php

D

Engagement Driver E
Personal Influence

You gain strength, courage and confidence by every experience
in which you really stop to look fear in the face.
You must do the thing you think you cannot do.
Eleanor Roosevelt – Human rights advocate
and First Lady of the United States

The Signpost

You don't recruit drones. You don't expect employees to disengage their brains when they enter the workplace. No, you want employees who think. Employees who proactively look for opportunities to improve the business, to increase productivity, to enhance quality, to generate breakthrough ideas. Employees who make a personal impact. So how are you actively promoting those behaviors and accomplishments in your workforce? Do your employees know their ideas count for something? Do they know they're making a difference? If not, your top talent will soon leave. And those who stay will contribute far below their potential.

Unskilled

- ☐ Fails to solicit ideas and input from workforce
- ☐ Does not acknowledge suggestions or provide timely feedback
- ☐ Implements unnecessarily restrictive policies and processes that stifle inventiveness
- ☐ Punishes risk takers and well-intentioned nonconformists
- ☐ Fails to communicate a clear vision and strategy for the organization
- ☐ Sends mixed signals regarding organizational values
- ☐ Delegates ineffectively; too directive or neglects to establish boundaries
- ☐ Fails to create a climate of trust
- ☐ Rewards status quo and compliance at the expense of accomplishments
- ☐ Makes exclusionary decisions; doesn't include broad set of stakeholders when appropriate

Skilled

- ☐ Clearly communicates vision, strategy, and values; explains the linkage to individual roles
- ☐ Celebrates creativity and risk taking; understands failures are part of learning

- [ ] Actively solicits employee input; establishes channels and processes for collecting employee suggestions
- [ ] Acknowledges suggestions, provides feedback, and makes related decisions all in a timely manner
- [ ] Coaches and mentors effectively; helps others learn from mistakes and failures
- [ ] Includes others in decision making, especially in decisions that impact their jobs
- [ ] Gives credit where credit is due; publicly recognizes and rewards initiative
- [ ] Eliminates bureaucratic nonsense, policies and procedures that stifle initiative
- [ ] Clearly sets expectations; empowers employees within defined boundaries
- [ ] Passionately creates a culture of teamwork and trust

Some Causes
- [ ] Poor listening
- [ ] Risk-averse culture
- [ ] Narcissistic management
- [ ] Pervasive distrust
- [ ] Lack of strategic clarity
- [ ] Inadequately developed team processes
- [ ] Lack of diversity and fresh perspectives
- [ ] Inadequate information sharing and transparency
- [ ] Rigid; slow to adapt
- [ ] Conflict avoidance

The Ten Leadership Architect® Competencies Most Associated with This Engagement Driver *(in order of connectedness)*

18. Delegation
33. Listening
53. *Drive for* Results
12. Conflict Management
46. Perspective
56. Sizing Up People
34. Managerial Courage
40. *Dealing with* Paradox
63. Total Work Systems (e.g., TQM/ISO/Six Sigma)
60. *Building Effective* Teams

The Map

Why are some employees willing to do so much more than required? To go the extra mile? To expend discretionary effort to serve the organization? To act on their convictions that they have personal influence and can truly make a difference? In any explanation, two factors loom large: confidence and satisfaction. To begin, employees need confidence that they have permission to act. The confidence that comes from being empowered to exercise independent thought, to think creatively, to make decisions and implement solutions within defined boundaries. Next, they need confidence that they have a reasonable chance of success. The confidence that comes from conscious competence. From an understanding of the issues and tasks they face on the job. From a firm grasp of the skills that will allow them to successfully resolve the issues and complete those tasks. To further bolster that, they also need confidence that occasional failures are not only allowed, they are expected. This doesn't refer to problem performers who struggle to meet minimum performance levels in their day-to-day jobs. It's about solid employees who make extra efforts, who take risks to do something good. They need confidence that they won't be punished if they've made an honest effort with less-than-stellar results. Another primary factor that contributes to employee engagement is satisfaction with outcomes. It's not enough to escape punishment. Employees need to feel the satisfaction that comes from acknowledgement of their efforts, from recognition of their willingness to try to achieve something of value for the organization. Even failed efforts need to be recognized—not for the failure, but for the good-faith attempt, the recognition that they gave it a good try. Suggestions submitted to management must at least be acknowledged, even if they are not implemented. They must be given reasonable consideration. Knowing that efforts are acknowledged and appreciated leads to satisfaction. And, of course, it should go without saying that successes should be celebrated, too. Confidence and satisfaction. Two factors that help employees gain a sense of personal influence, to believe they are important, that they make a difference, that they are really heard by people who matter, and that they add value that's recognized by others. These are factors that drive engagement and are largely impacted by organizational leadership. Confident employees who find satisfaction in their work and possess a genuine sense of personal influence will run circles around employees who don't. The payoff for organizations that have employees so engaged is tremendous.

Some Remedies

☐ **1. Clearly link strategy, vision, mission, and values to key roles.** Communicate frequently and precisely about where the organization is going, how it plans to get there, and what values are critical to success. Let people know why their contribution is important, why their job matters, how they fit into the value chain. The assembly-line employee installing seat belts can view her job as installing fasteners or as saving lives. The proofreader at a publisher can view his job as correcting typos or as educating thousands. The point of view will distinctly impact levels of engagement. So provide a purpose. Communicate the big picture. Describe the highest goals of your organization in terms of value provided to the customer. Make the focus crystal clear so employees really understand it and feel it in their core. Finely craft the message to capture the essence of what really matters in your organization. State it simply so it's accessible to all levels. Customize the message to engage different audiences. Tell stories that reinforce your message. Stories about teams and individual employees who have gone the extra mile to please a customer. Stories about those who took the initiative to implement an improvement that impacted the bottom line. Help individual managers to connect the dots for their teams so no one in the organization is confused or ambivalent about their role.

☐ **2. Give employees a sandbox.** A sandbox is a place to dig in. A place to create. A place to have fun. And a primary job of management is to make sure that the jobs—the sandboxes—in the organization are designed well and defined clearly for employees. Effective delegation is a key part of that process. Effective delegation spells out the desired outcome, the accomplishments that define success. Effective delegation defines the boundaries within which employees do the job, exercise judgment, and have authority to make decisions. While it's important to clearly define desired outcomes, it's usually less important to define how the outcomes are achieved. Consider the capabilities of employees and provide only as much direction on how to achieve results as they need. Allow them to think, to be creative, to exercise discretion, to figure things out. To the extent possible, set goals and schedules collaboratively. Give support as needed, but don't get in the way. Give people room to do the job. Minimize control and bureaucracy. Provide them with meaningful work, the tools and resources they need to be successful, and an enabling environment. If there are performance problems or a lack of engagement, the root cause is likely due to something in management's control. Management defines the nature of jobs. Management communicates requirements. Management provides tools and resources. And management is responsible for the work environment. If management is not attending to these things, it's failing.

☐ **3. Broaden the idea pipeline.** Who are the innovators in your organization? Where are they? Do you believe innovation is limited to key people or specific functions such as R&D or marketing? If so, expand your thinking! Everyone has ideas. Everyone has the potential to provide important suggestions that can drive organizational performance. Does everyone in the organization know their ideas are valued? That their suggestions are needed? Does everyone have a simple means of submitting suggestions? The easiest way to get ideas is to ask for them. Loud and clear. Employees should hear the request from top management as well as the immediate boss. Ask. And take the time to listen. Listen to suggestions. Listen to opinions. Listen to concerns. Really listen. Provide a formalized process for employees to submit their ideas. The submission process should be nearly effortless for the employee. Add informal programs and initiatives to demonstrate that the organization listens to and values employee suggestions. Conduct focus groups. Schedule skip-level lunches to give employees time to personally interact with senior leaders. Hold listening-post sessions with employees and, in return for providing juice and bagels, discover new ideas to drive the business forward. Employees don't expect every idea to be implemented, but they want to be heard. And organizations that put in the time and effort to listen to employees will benefit from increased engagement, higher retention, and innovative solutions that will enhance the business.

☐ **4. Act decisively on suggestions.** When you open the floodgates for suggestions from the workforce, you better be prepared. Prepared to acknowledge suggestions quickly. Prepared to quickly review them and make implementation decisions. Prepared to give substantive feedback to the employee. Depending on the size of your workforce, you may need one or more full-time people to manage this process. Someone needs to quickly acknowledge the suggestion and set expectations about the time frame for reviewing and making related decisions. It's demoralizing for an employee to be encouraged to submit ideas but then have suggestions fall into a black hole. So acknowledge them quickly. Forward suggestions to the person or persons who can assess the value of the suggestion, can make decisions, and can commit resources to implement sound ideas. Act quickly. Provide meaningful feedback, especially when the suggestion is not accepted. Give rationale for not adopting the suggestion as well as sincere thanks for the effort put into making the suggestion.

☐ **5. Make everyone who suggests an improvement accountable to some degree for that improvement.** An employee makes a great suggestion. Now what? Do you pass it off to another department or cross-functional team to implement? What role does the employee who made the suggestion play?

Are they out of the loop once the suggestion is submitted? Better that they have a role, a key role if possible, in implementing the suggestion. Some suggestions are more insightful than others. Some are much more specific and actionable than others. When employees know that they are likely to bear some accountability for implementing suggestions, they're much more likely to make specific, actionable suggestions that are smaller in scope. That's a good thing! It's easy to make grand and sweeping suggestions. Adopt a pay-for-performance program. Implement an ERP or CRM application. Reorganize the business around key customer segments. All these might be good ideas that will truly pay off for the organization, but each is also a massive undertaking requiring loads of resources and management bandwidth. It's likely that an employee who makes such a suggestion will not be in a position to play the primary role in the implementation of the idea. On the other hand, some suggestions are specific and very actionable. Change the temperature of parts washing fluid to save energy. Make the design of a part asymmetrical for foolproof installation. Adopt an easier-to-follow format for product installation instructions. Create a simplified warranty registration process. These are improvements that might be managed by the person who makes the suggestion. Give them that opportunity. If an employee submits a good idea, make every effort to authorize them to take the lead on implementing the solution. That will truly empower them. It will enhance their sense of personal influence. And, when all is said and done, will more fully engage them.

☐ **6. Create a participatory culture that promotes calculated risk taking.** Your organization's culture impacts the way decisions are made, the way work gets done, how communication flows, how people are hired and promoted—just about every aspect of day-to-day work. To establish a sense of personal influence in employees, start with decision making. The most direct way for them to feel a sense of personal influence is to include them in decisions, especially those that affect their jobs. Employees are more likely to accept and be committed to decisions when they are part of the process, even if their view is not the winning one. The more a decision directly impacts employees, the more they should be involved. An added benefit is that participative decision making provides on-the-job training for developing skills such as problem solving, decision quality, and conflict management. Participative decision making as a process can be formal, as in task forces, consultative committees, and focus groups. Or informal, as it occurs in a chat with the boss in the lunchroom or an impromptu hallway discussion. Risk orientation is another key aspect of culture. Playing it safe is not a path to innovation and empowerment. Neither is being reckless. Find the balance that promotes calculated risk taking. Develop methods for risk analysis and to define risk thresholds based on the impact of the decision, good or bad. Teach employees to assess risks and how to set confidence levels that are factored into decisions. It takes a certain amount of management humility to listen and be receptive to ideas from the rank and file, to allow them to participate in decisions. It takes management restraint to turn loose, to give up control and allow employees to pursue risky initiatives. And it takes a certain amount of management selflessness to give credit and recognize others. Management humility, restraint, and selflessness are hallmarks of participative, innovative, and risk-taking cultures. Publicly support employee decisions that are well-thought-out and stand behind employees as they experiment with new things. Nothing stifles initiative more than continually being second-guessed. Recognize people who take appropriate risks. Recognize valiant attempts that end in failure. Send a clear message that there is amnesty for reasonable, calculated risks that don't pan out. Sometimes the greatest leaps forward in innovation come from learning what not to do. So treat the organization like a classroom and involve everyone in continuous learning.

☐ **7. Support self-managed teams.** Winning organizations know how to tap into the expertise of their people. They know how to leverage that expertise by bringing them together to work in self-managed work teams. Quality circles. Cross-functional teams. Action-learning assignments. Project teams set up to solve specific problems. There are plenty of opportunities. Look around for low-hanging fruit and tap the right individuals to serve in team roles. Don't get hung up on job titles, functions, or levels. In fact, the more diverse the team, the more diverse the thought process will likely be. Implement process engineering programs that empower people to continually reinvent more effective ways of doing business. Reduce organizational gridlock. Allow people to get obstacles out of the way so they can do their work better. It's a winning situation all around. The organization will benefit from a continuous flow of improvement and innovation. In turn, employees will develop critical skills such as conflict management, problem solving, and business acumen. And their level of engagement will increase as they see their personal influence grow and they make meaningful contributions to the success of the organization.

☐ **8. Teach essential skills.** Learning is acquiring the ability to do something new, something different. People learn, of course, but so do organizations. Some better than others. Effective learning organizations change readily. They adapt to new methods. They create knowledge, organize it, share it, and protect it. They tolerate, even celebrate, mistakes because they treat them as an opportunity for learning. They embed knowledge management into their systems and embrace change. Relentlessly promote organizational learning. Instill a passion for learning in the workforce. Teach the differentiating, mission-critical competencies that specifically apply to your organization. Teach analytical methods. Teach the business drivers for your firm. Teach problem-solving and decision-making techniques and involve employees at every level in action-learning projects with real implications. As employees develop critical skills, they'll also be making meaningful improvements for the organization. Teach delegation skills to managers. Delegation is a key method of empowering the workforce, and it frees up management time for additional value-adding work. Train managers in collaboration, team building, conflict management, group facilitation skills, and developing peer relations. All these skills will help them empower the workforce and optimize engagement.

☐ **9. Recognize and celebrate individual efforts and accomplishments.** Show employees that the organization values their ideas by publicly acknowledging them. Recognize individual employees and teams for ideas, suggestions, innovative solutions, and meaningful accomplishments. Publicly recognize initiative-taking that helps the organization. Be very cautious about implementing a formal compensation plan to reward suggestions. Better to infuse your culture with an expectation of individual suggestions and contributions at all levels. Strengthen appropriate behaviors with intangible reinforcement—it's free and it's effective. Research studies confirm the effectiveness of spontaneous recognition from the immediate boss. Pats on the back, words of praise, and handwritten notes—all have incredible meaning to employees. Celebrations, too, are important ways to reinforce the right behaviors and strengthen your culture. For instance, monthly luncheons with senior leadership to recognize outstanding teams and individuals can be very motivating. If you do choose to reward employee initiative and suggestions with tangible reinforcement, consider non-cash spot bonuses. A pair of movie tickets or a gift certificate to a nice restaurant, for example, can be effective to recognize extraordinary ideas, efforts, and accomplishments. Provide feedback, too, to help employees grow and to reinforce the importance of their contributions. Teach employees to gauge the quality of suggestions so there is continuous improvement in the quality of suggestions submitted. This will also help them understand and accept when their ideas are not implemented and keep them in the game, keep them engaged.

☐ **10. Enhance your management selection criteria.** What do you look for when hiring a manager? Are you assessing the right competencies in your interviews? Studies show that most managers who fail lack personal and interpersonal skills. Listening. Understanding others. Developing others. Building effective teams. Motivating others. These are some of the leadership skills that are in short supply and also most related to empowering others. It's generally more important to look for skills like these in management candidates than for skills that are in high supply, such as intellectual horsepower, business acumen, and drive for results. When choosing between multiple candidates with roughly equivalent qualifications and accomplishments, favor the one with the best people skills. Design a rigorous selection process to ensure you get the right people in the key management positions that will impact performance and engagement.

*The people who are doing the work are the moving force behind
the Macintosh. My job is to create a space for them,
to clear out the rest of the organization and keep it at bay.*
Steve Jobs – Cofounder and CEO, Apple Computer

Suggested Readings

Ashkenas, R., Kerr, S., & Ulrich, D. (2002). *The GE work-out: How to implement GE's revolutionary method for busting bureaucracy and attacking organizational problems fast.* NY: McGraw-Hill.

Black, J. S., & Gregersen, H. B. (1997). Participative decision making: An integration of multiple dimensions. *Human Relations, 50,* 859-878.

Case, J. (1996). *Open-book management: The coming business revolution.* NY: HarperCollins.

Drake, S., Gulman, M. J., & Roberts, S. (2005). *Light their fire: Using internal marketing to ignite employee performance and wow your customers.* Chicago: Dearborn Trade: A Kaplan Company.

Ginnodo, B. (Ed.). (1997). *The power of empowerment: What the experts say and 16 actionable case studies.* Arlington Heights, IL: Pride Publications.

Heathfield, S. M. (2007). *Top ten ways to make employee empowerment fail.* Retrieved January 15, 2009, from http://humanresources.about.com/od/involvementteams/a/empowerment.htm?p=1

Houlihan, A. (2007). Empower your employees to make smart decisions. *Supervision, 68*(7), 3-5.

Industrial Relations Victoria. (2006, November). *Workplace consultation: Employee participation in decision making.* Library No. 60037. Victoria, Australia: Department of Innovation, Industry, and Regional Development.

Kanter, R. M. (1989). The new managerial work. *Harvard Business Review, 67*(6), 85-92.

Koberg, C. S., Boss, W. R., Senjem, J. C., & Goodman, E. A. (1999). Antecedents and outcomes of empowerment. *Group & Organization Management, 24*(1), 71-91.

Locke, E. A., Schweiger, D. M., & Latham, G. P. (1986). Participation in decision making: When should it be used? *Organizational Dynamics, 14*(3), 65-79.

McShane, S. L., & Von Glinow, M. A. (2008). *Organizational behavior: Emerging realities for the workplace revolution* (4th ed.). NY: McGraw-Hill/Irwin.

Mishra, J. M. (1994). Employee suggestion programs in the health care field: The rewards of involvement. *Public Personnel Management, 23*(4), 587-593.

Murrell, K. L., & Meredith, M. (2000). *Empowering employees.* NY: McGraw-Hill.

Nelson, B. (1994). *1001 Ways to reward employees.* NY: Workman Publishing.

Nichols, D. (1989). Bottom-up strategies: Asking the employees for advice. *Management Review, 78*(12), 44-50.

Parnell, J. A., & Menefee, M. (1995). The business strategy-employee involvement contingency: The impact of strategy-participation fit on performance. *American Business Review, 13*, 90-100.

Pierce, J. L., O'Driscoll, M. P., & Coghlan, A. (2004). Work environment structure and psychological ownership: The mediating effects of control. *Journal of Social Psychology, 144*, 507-534.

Robinson, A. G., & Schroeder, D. M. (2006). *Ideas are free: How the idea revolution is liberating people and transforming organizations.* San Francisco: Berrett-Koehler.

Sirota, D., Mischkind, L. A., & Meltzer, M. I. (2005). *The enthusiastic employee: How companies profit by giving workers what they want.* Upper Saddle River, NJ: Pearson Education.

Swindall, C. (2007). *Engaged leadership: Building a culture to overcome employee disengagement.* Hoboken, NJ: John Wiley & Sons.

Tjosvold, D. (1998). Making employee involvement work: Cooperative goals and controversy to reduce costs. *Human Relations, 51*, 201-215.

Tracy, D. (1992). *Ten steps to empowerment: A common-sense guide to managing people.* NY: HarperCollins.

E

Engagement Driver F
Nature of My Career

For many people a job is more than an income—it's an important part of who we are. So a career transition of any sort is one of the most unsettling experiences you can face in your life.
Paul Clitheroe – Financial analyst and television journalist

The Signpost
Talented individuals want more than a job. They want a career. A job pays today's bills. But a career is about the future. About lifelong learning and development. About making a contribution over the long haul. About meeting long-range financial goals. A career is so much more than a job. A career path will engage your employees, especially your high-potential talent. So, how well have you defined and communicated career paths in your organization?

Unskilled
- ☐ Fails to identify and communicate key roles and associated career paths
- ☐ Restricts internal job moves within silos or to linear career paths
- ☐ Holds talented people in jobs for too long
- ☐ Judges talent poorly; frequently makes poor hiring and promotion decisions
- ☐ Leaves business units and functions to manage talent on their own
- ☐ Allows line managers to interfere with moving people across business units
- ☐ Doesn't proactively engage top leadership in succession management
- ☐ Fails to achieve appropriate ratio of internal promotions to new hires from outside
- ☐ Ignores the importance of creating a strong employment brand
- ☐ Gives insufficient time and effort to job design and career management

Skilled
- ☐ Creates and communicates a compelling employment brand
- ☐ Identifies key competencies and roles for associated career paths
- ☐ Considers demographic trends and workforce values when defining career options
- ☐ Offers multiple career tracks for technical professionals and general managers

- ☐ Excels at talent assessment and talent deployment decisions
- ☐ Engages top management and board levels in talent management
- ☐ Fills most senior jobs with successful candidates from inside the organization
- ☐ Values and promotes diversity of perspectives and backgrounds
- ☐ Links executive and management incentives/compensation to talent goals
- ☐ Celebrates and highlights career success

Some Causes

- ☐ Narrow perspective; one-dimensional view of career progression
- ☐ Inadequate development of human capital strategy
- ☐ Insufficient resources devoted to talent management
- ☐ Short-term mentality
- ☐ Organizational barriers; functional silos
- ☐ Leader insecurity; defensiveness
- ☐ Complacency; doesn't consider career management important
- ☐ Weak, unsophisticated HR function
- ☐ Inconsistent criteria for promotions
- ☐ Unorganized; poor planning

The Ten Leadership Architect® Competencies Most Associated with This Engagement Driver *(in order of connectedness)*

56. Sizing Up People
19. Developing Direct Reports and Others
36. Motivating Others
58. Strategic Agility
33. Listening
52. Process Management
20. Directing Others
65. *Managing* Vision and Purpose
18. Delegation
47. Planning

The Map

Getting ahead. Wanting to grow. Progressing. Having more responsibility. More authority. More accountability. Making more money. Securing a financial future into retirement. Building a legacy. These are not objectives uniquely held by those destined for a corner office. They are widely held goals for people of all ages. They are the stuff of careers. And though many employees don't have the capability and motivation to advance into a role in the C-suite, a great many do have an intense and genuine interest in a meaningful career, something that significantly contributes to their identity and sense of purpose. Such employees really matter. In a period of deepening talent shortages, you really can't afford to lose them. It is well worth the time and effort and resources required to design and communicate career paths in your organization that provide employees with options. Several roads can lead to the same destination. Some are relatively straight. But most are twisting and have many branches, side trips that enrich the journey, side trips that provide variety and opportunities for learning and growth. Become a mapmaker. You'll never be able to identify all the possible routes, but you can certainly chart out major career paths and plot optional tracks that lead to the key positions in your organization. You can describe the career journeys of a sampling of leaders in your organization to demonstrate the importance of key developmental assignments and illustrate the variety of routes available. Communicating those career paths and stories of how leaders in your organization got to where they are will engage and challenge and inspire your workforce. Create believable maps and stories that point to the future. Design meaningful career paths loaded with important jobs and challenging developmental assignments. Career paths that support diversity. Career paths that are navigated by merit. The organizations that do this well engage talent. They hang on to talent. In the competition for talent, they are the winners.

Some Remedies

☐ **1. Create a compelling employment brand.** What attracts talent to your organization? Why do talented people want to stay? A well-developed employment brand answers those questions and creates an image of your firm in the minds of current and prospective employees, customers, and the community. Create an employment brand as part of a long-term talent management strategy. Align the employment brand with your organization's vision, mission, core values, and product/service branding initiatives. All these elements should be complementary and paint a complete picture about what it's like to work for your firm. To be effective, the brand should evoke memorable images and stories that make your target audience want to rush to submit a resume. Some of those stories are sure to speak to the future and the nature of careers in your firm. If you've done a good job designing career paths, those images and stories will not be difficult to create.

☐ **2. Think strategically about careers when designing the organization.** The design of your organization should support your strategic goals and the business processes created to deliver value to your customers. Organization design is a messy business. It's not a linear or sequential process. Organization design, process engineering, development of talent management practices, and creation of policies and procedures all follow strategy development and, more or less, are done concurrently. The design of your organization will largely define the types of jobs and career paths in your organization. Take that into consideration as you're making organization design decisions the same way you consider alignment with business processes and talent management practices. Be explicit about your career strategy. Get top management involved so they own the strategy and can speak about it clearly. There is no substitute for the active and visible support of top management. Your employees, especially your high-potential talent, will watch and listen to top management to learn their views about the future and discover career opportunities. Those employees need to know that top management spends time and energy thinking about the future and cares about providing career opportunities. All talent management best practices follow top management involvement.

☐ **3. Identify key jobs.** Some roles in your organization are more important than others, and it's not about position level. It's about competitive differentiation. Key jobs are the jobs that give your organization competitive advantage. Jobs that are closely aligned with your strategy and mission. These jobs, when done well, contribute more to the company's success than other jobs. Key jobs demand special skills—technical and/or leadership skills—that are in short supply. The required skill sets are not easy to develop. They're tough for your competitors to replicate, and that's where you gain your edge. Take the time to identify these jobs. They should be the dots that are connected by the most significant career paths in your organization. These jobs should command your attention. They should be staffed strategically. Don't be fooled by complex jobs typically done by professionals but that aren't differentiating. Most organizations employ professionals in functions such as finance, information technology, and legal departments. These are complex jobs that require advanced education. They may be assigned a high position level. And they may be corporate staff roles. They are important roles, to be sure, but they're typically not the jobs that provide competitive advantage. Get clear about this. The people in your key jobs, the jobs that are both differentiating and complex, are the true royalty class in your organization. You should be broadcasting that fact, not keeping it a secret.

☐ **4. Map out career paths.** Start with the top leadership positions and key jobs in the organization. Map out several possible career paths that lead to each of those leadership positions and key roles. Consider the experiences required to be successful in those roles. Make sure that every path has clearly defined developmental assignments—jobs that provide stretch and development in the competencies that are most critical for the organization. These development jobs fall into two categories. Industry-specific developmental assignments provide opportunities to learn technical or specialized skills that don't completely transfer to other businesses. These can also fill the bill when there are expectations in your organization that certain leadership roles will only be filled by people that have had exposure to various functions. For instance, there might be an unwritten rule that no one will become chief operating officer without having had assignments in finance, marketing, and manufacturing. The other type of developmental jobs teaches general leadership skills that are readily transferred. These are jobs such as start-ups, turnarounds, and international assignments. They have been studied by the Center for Creative Leadership and outlined in the book *The Lessons of Experience*. People learn primarily from experience, and these jobs are the building blocks for certain key competencies and skills needed for future leaders. Make sure they're included in the career paths leading to your top positions.

☐ **5. Accurately assess and differentiate talent.** To be fair, your employees should be evaluated on performance and potential and provided feedback that will help them realistically assess their options. For general management roles, you need people high in learning agility. People who learn from experience. Who can transfer learning to new situations. People who can easily adapt. Change. Those qualities are not nearly as critical for most technical and professional roles. Research has shown that typical line managers have difficulty making tough calls on potential. Potential is not the same as performance. That's an erroneous connection most managers make, and it decreases the accuracy of the calls on potential. Teach your managers the difference and help them learn to accurately assess both performance and potential. This is important so you can customize your treatment of talent. Your talented professionals on a technical career path are different from those on a general management career path. They need to be treated differently. Different development. Different incentives. Different opportunities. Different careers.

☐ **6. Implement appropriate visibility in the succession management process.** Put transparency into your succession planning process. Your people, particularly the most career-minded, need a glimpse into the process. They want to see periodic activity and communication related to succession planning. At the very least, they should have a discussion about their own performance and potential with their boss. Better yet, they should be the topic of a discussion among a group of multilevel leaders familiar with their work. Those discussions, in addition to addressing performance and potential, should include developmental assignments, readiness for next step, and long-term potential. Employees will see a future career at your firm if they observe the firm is planning for the future. This is not to say every detail of the succession plan must be public. Most organizations don't have the talent management sophistication and culture to allow the names of high-potential candidates to be publicized, for instance, without creating problems for those who don't make the list. So some information should definitely be kept confidential. But here is the key—the process itself should be understood and accessible by all interested employees. Make sure you reach down into the organization with your succession planning, too. Drop the lure all the way to the bottom in addition to trolling just below the surface. If your succession plan stops at the director level, for instance, you will be missing an opportunity to do deliberate career planning for talented people in their 20s and 30s. Not only will they not receive developmental assignments and coaching, they won't know it's available. And they'll likely leave. Or, perhaps worse, they'll stay and feel stifled. The best firms understand that it takes 15 to 20 years of challenging, diverse experiences to build the competencies and confidence needed to become an effective executive.

☐ **7. Design jobs that engage.** Employee engagement increases when employees are in jobs that appropriately challenge them. Of course, you'll naturally consider the needs of the business when designing jobs. But don't neglect the needs of the workforce. When a well-designed job is staffed with the right person, the employee will have a highly favorable view of these factors:

- *Information:* There is clear communication about expectations and feedback on performance.
- *Task Variety:* The job provides an opportunity to use a variety of skills.
- *Importance:* The job delivers something important to others.
- *Freedom:* There is an appropriate level of independence afforded in doing the job.

Even if you've attended to these factors when designing a job, you'll still have a disengaged employee if you do a poor job of selection when hiring. What constitutes meaningful information, task variety, job importance, and freedom differs from one person to another. You can err in either direction—by setting the selection bar too low or too high. Too low and you've got major problems on your hands—employees who, even if motivated, deliver poor performance and lack the capability of ever developing the skills the job requires. Too high and you'll soon have engagement issues because the intrinsic motivation isn't there. You've got great talent on the bus, but the ride is never going to please the overqualified employee unless you change the job to fit the employee. Put lots of thought into job design so the right work gets done the right way by the right employees. When you do, you'll get better quality, better productivity, and a more engaged workforce.

☐ **8. Accelerate career movement for your top talent.** The majority of skill and perspective building comes from going through a series of challenging jobs and experiences. Research indicates that high potentials generally need about eight jobs to acquire the skills needed to take on a high-level general management position. The duration of each job should be between about 24 and 36 months. Assignments shorter than that don't teach much. Assignments longer than that run out of things that teach. Jobs can build both skills and perspective. There are assignments that just build perspective and some that just build skills. The plum jobs are those that teach both—a start-up outside the person's home country, for example. Ideally, your top talent will go through a series of about eight jobs that are matched with their specific developmental and career needs. Not everyone needs to manage a start-up. Not everyone needs to work out of their home country. Your people, especially your high potentials, will benefit from knowing that a system is in place to keep them moving through key developmental assignments. The end result will be engaged and retained talent.

☐ **9. Accommodate exit and reentry into the career path.** Nowadays, career predictability is out. Career flexibility is in. Many people need to take a break from their career. Men. Women. Young employees. Older employees. All position levels. For a variety of reasons, people temporarily exit their career path. Child care. Elder care. Education. Military service. Significant life events. Or to fulfill some personal goal or agenda. Career sabbaticals can be energizing and times of great personal growth. They can benefit both the individual and, in the long-term, the organization. Organizations that are flexible, supportive, and respectful of the individual will be more successful in finding, engaging, and retaining the talent they need. Accommodate those individuals who need to temporarily leave their career path for whatever reason. Respect their decision. If you value their contribution, do as much as possible to assist their reentry and return to their chosen career path.

☐ **10. Institutionalize success stories.** Everyone likes a good rags-to-riches story. The urban myth (and occasional reality) of working up from the mailroom to the boardroom still exists. Seeing the long shot or the underdog succeed through a combination of skill and perseverance is inspiring to us all. So, when this happens in your own backyard, take advantage of it and let people know. They'll get insight into what it actually takes to succeed within the organization over the long-term. They'll understand that successful careers often include jobs that weren't glamorous but were essential in teaching critical skills. They'll be encouraged to think, "Hey, that could be me someday." What's more inspiring than hearing about the girl who started peddling newspapers and rose to become publisher of the newspaper or the boy who started flipping burgers and rose to become CEO of a huge fast-food chain. Those stories illustrate more than the moxie of the youngster. They are a testament to the organization's savvy approach to talent development and succession planning. They will inspire and engage your employees.

> *It is extremely unlikely that anyone coming out of school with a*
> *technical degree will go into one area and stay there.*
> *Today's students have to look forward to the excitement of*
> *probably having three or four careers.*
> Gordon Moore – Cofounder, former Chairman
> and CEO, Intel Corporation

F

Suggested Readings

Arnold, J., & Davey, K. M. (1999). Graduates' work experiences as predictors of organizational commitment, intention to leave, and turnover: Which experiences really matter? *Applied Psychology: An International Review, 48,* 211-238.

Ashkenas, R., Ulrich, D., Jick, T., & Kerr, S. (1995). *The boundaryless organization: Breaking the chains of organizational structure.* San Francisco: Jossey-Bass.

Ball, B., & Jordan, M. (1997). An open-learning approach to career management and guidance. *British Journal of Guidance & Counseling, 25,* 507-517.

Baruch, Y., & Peiperl, M. (2000). Career management practices: An empirical survey and implications. *Human Resource Management, 39,* 347-366.

Brousseau, K. R., Driver, M. J., Eneroth, K., & Larsson, R. (1996). Career pandemonium: Realigning organizations and individuals. *Academy of Management Executive, 10,* 52-66.

Brown, D. (2007). *Career information, career counseling, and career development* (9th ed.). Needham Heights, MA: Allyn & Bacon.

Cappelli, P., & Cascio, W. F. (1991). Why some jobs command wage premiums: A test of career tournament and internal labor market hypotheses. *Academy of Management Journal, 34,* 848-868.

Cawood, S., & Bailey, R. V. (2006). *Destination profit: Creating people-profit opportunities in your organization.* Mountain View, CA: Davies-Black.

Deal, J. J. (2007). *Retiring the generation gap: How employees young and old can find common ground: Center for Creative Leadership.* San Francisco: Jossey-Bass.

Eby, L. T., Allen, T. D., & Brinley, A. (2005). A cross-level investigation of the relationship between career management practices and career-related attitudes. *Group & Organization Management, 30,* 565-596.

Eichinger, R. W., Lombardo, M. M., & Ulrich, D. (2004). *100 Things you need to know: Best people practices for managers & HR.* Minneapolis, MN: Lominger International: A Korn/Ferry Company.

Feldman, D. C. (1988). *Managing careers in organizations.* Glenview, IL: Scott Foresman.

Feldman, D. C. (1995). The impact of downsizing on organizational career development activities and employee career development opportunities. *Human Resource Management Review, 5,* 189-221.

Greenhaus, J. H., Callanan, G. A., & Godshalk, V. M. (2000). *Career management* (3rd ed.). Fort Worth, TX: Dryden Press.

Gutteridge, T. G., & Otte, F. L. (1983). Organizational career development: What's going on out there? *Training and Development Journal, 37*(2), 22-26.

Joinson, C. (2001). Employee sculpt thyself...with a little help. *HR Magazine, 46*(5), 60-65.

Kaye, B. (2002). *Up is not the only way: A guide to developing workforce talent* (2nd ed.). Palo Alto, CA: Davies-Black.

Knowdell, R. L. (1996). *Building a career development program: Nine steps for effective implementation.* Palo Alto, CA: Davies-Black.

Kummerow, J. (2000). *New directions in career planning and the workplace* (2nd ed.). Palo Alto, CA: Davies-Black.

Lips-Wiersma, M., & Hall, D. T. (2007). Organizational career development is not dead: A case study on managing the new career during organizational change. *Journal of Organizational Behavior, 28,* 771-792.

Mallon, M., & Walton, S. (2005). Career and learning: The ins and the outs of it. *Personnel Review, 34,* 468-487.

McCall, M. W., Lombardo, M. M., & Morrison, A. M. (1988). *The lessons of experience: How successful executives develop on the job.* NY: Free Press.

Nelson, B. (1997). *1001 Ways to energize employees.* NY: Workman.

Niles, S. G., & Harris-Bowlsbey, J. (2004). *Career development interventions in the 21st century* (2nd ed.). Upper Saddle River, NJ: Prentice Hall.

Rothwell, W. J., Jackson, R. D., Knight, S. C., & Lindholm, J. E. (2005). *Career planning and succession management: Developing your organization's talent—for today and tomorrow.* Westport, CT: Praeger.

Sullivan, S. E. (1999). The changing nature of careers: A review and research agenda. *Journal of Management, 25,* 457-484.

Van Maanen, J., & Schein, E. H. (1979). Toward a theory of organizational socialization. In B. M. Staw (Ed.), *Research in organizational behavior* (Vol. 1, pp. 206-264). Greenwich, CT: JAI.

F

Engagement Driver G
Career Support

The people who get on in this world are the people who get up and look
for the circumstances they want, and if they can't find them, make them.
George Bernard Shaw – Irish playwright and
Nobel Prize winner for Literature

The Signpost
Winning organizations need people who have the capability and desire to grow. They need people who can adapt to meet the strategic needs of the business. Finding and recruiting those talented people is challenging, but the challenge isn't over once they're on the payroll. Your top talent wants a meaningful, supported career path. Top talent wants to be stretched. Top talent wants attention and support. Typical managers are notoriously poor at developing people. How much commitment do your leaders have to nurturing talent? To providing career support? How much time do they devote to it? Do they make key jobs and developmental assignments available for top talent?

Unskilled
- ☐ Fails to provide visible top management support for career development
- ☐ Places low priority on career management; line management doesn't make time for meaningful dialogue
- ☐ Lacks ability to accurately assess talent, especially high-potential talent
- ☐ Blocks line of sight to succession management process; conceals process from most employees
- ☐ Ignores long-term potential and developmental needs to focus on current performance
- ☐ Deploys talent without considering developmental opportunities; solely considers operational needs of the business
- ☐ Doesn't understand basics of career development; unaware of available career paths
- ☐ Neglects to provide career feedback and coaching
- ☐ Allows line managers to interfere with development assignments to keep key talent
- ☐ Fails to commit resources to develop formal career development programs

G

Skilled

- ☐ Visibly engages top management in career development
- ☐ Establishes metrics to gauge effectiveness of career support; holds line management accountable
- ☐ Broadly communicates career paths, resources, and options
- ☐ Commits resources to bolster career support; employs internal and external resources
- ☐ Effectively provides career-related coaching and feedback; has meaningful career conversations
- ☐ Reinforces employee initiative and self-directed career development
- ☐ Implements high-quality training strategically focused on critical, differentiating skills
- ☐ Excels at talent assessment and talent deployment decisions
- ☐ Regularly collects information from employees to learn what they value and want from their careers
- ☐ Pays attention to employee integration; implements a comprehensive onboarding process

Some Causes

- ☐ Inability to accurately size up people
- ☐ Failure to listen
- ☐ Inattentive to details and execution
- ☐ Conflict avoidance
- ☐ Short-term mentality
- ☐ Favoritism and/or nepotism
- ☐ Failure to discriminate performance levels and treat people differently
- ☐ Organizational barriers; functional silos
- ☐ Insufficient investment in talent
- ☐ Narrow perspective; short-term view

The Ten Leadership Architect® Competencies Most Associated with This Engagement Driver *(in order of connectedness)*

33. Listening
19. Developing Direct Reports and Others
13. Confronting Direct Reports
56. Sizing Up People
12. Conflict Management
7. Caring About Direct Reports
18. Delegation

23. Fairness to Direct Reports
36. Motivating Others
58. Strategic Agility

The Map

Who's really responsible for career development? Aren't employees responsible? Shouldn't individuals be proactive and take control of their own destiny? Shouldn't they independently pursue development opportunities that will propel their career toward their long-term goal? Yes, of course they should. But what about organizations? Don't organizations benefit when individuals learn new skills? Shouldn't organizations support employees with resources and programs to enhance their competencies and manage careers? Yes, of course they should. The truth is, both individuals and organizations have lots to gain from committing resources and energy into managing careers. From the employee perspective, it's easy to see. Energy and drive are readily observable and have historically been rewarded by managers. The eager beaver who arrives to work early, stays late, signs up for extracurricular development, and is always ready to please is a dream employee for most managers. That route to advancement, the Horatio Alger version of the rags-to-riches story, has been touted for many years as the way to get ahead. Nothing wrong with energy and drive as long as managers don't use motivation as the sole criterion for promotion. Accomplishments trump activity. Accomplishments are what matter. And you probably have many employees who have greater potential to scale career heights than do your eager beavers. They're the employees who quietly produce meaningful accomplishments. They're skilled and efficient but don't wear their motivation on their sleeve. And they're the ones who especially benefit when your organization provides career support. Sometimes all it takes is a little spark of enablement to get the engine running full speed. Meaningful conversations about career possibilities. The offer of career counseling and tuition assistance. Managers who take an interest. Next thing you know, the highly capable employees who may have been lukewarm about their careers are charging ahead to pursue opportunities and plan their future with the organization. They're growing. Learning new skills. Dynamically filling your talent pipeline. Infusing the organization with energy. Driving the business forward as they put their careers into overdrive. That's absolutely a win-win situation. Organizations that understand this don't hesitate to provide career support. It engages. It pays.

Some Remedies

☐ **1. Engage top management in talent management and career support.** Research is crystal clear. Nothing much happens unless top management is truly committed to talent management. Employees need to see that commitment. Active commitment. Visible commitment. Senior executives who set the agenda and drive the pace of development. Senior executives who model career development. It's your senior leadership team that creates the culture. Senior leadership commits the resources. They won't (or can't) do that if they don't really see the importance of talent. They won't do it if they're tactically diverted with operational firefighting. Do what it takes to educate the top leaders so they really get it. So they understand that "our people are our most important asset" is more than a cliché. So they understand that people truly are the source of almost all competitive advantage. Put talent management on the agenda. Make it top of mind. Ensure that top executives engage in career discussions and provide feedback to their direct reports and several levels deeper in the organization. Assign members of top management to mentor up-and-coming high potentials. Take special care to recruit a highly skilled and respected person into your top talent management role. Someone who has credibility with top management. Someone who is a master at influencing others. A master at facilitating change. Make talent management one leg of your strategy stool. Address it prominently in your annual report and other key communications.

☐ **2. Start career development on day one.** Sign these forms. There's your desk. Restrooms are down the hall to the left. Sound typical? Unfortunately, many employees don't get much more than that as an introduction to a new job. Much better to implement a robust onboarding program that integrates them into their new job and organization and lays the groundwork for success. Career support should be part of that robust program. Start career discussions very soon, even before the first day, if possible. Make sure new employees get acquainted with the key jobs, career paths, and the available career resources. And make sure the organization gets acquainted with the new employee, too. You assessed their capabilities during the selection process. Don't lose that assessment. Use it as a starting point for further assessment and discovery about their talents and career goals in the first few months of employment. As you learn more about strengths, weaknesses, and career aspirations, incorporate the information in career planning. Maintain an ongoing dialogue with the employee to keep apprised of how things are going, what's working, what's not working. Modify the support provided to leverage the talent, to give them confidence, to make them successful—in the short-term as well as far into the future.

☐ **3. Match career paths with the unique capabilities and aspirations of individuals.** Map out several possible career paths that lead to the top leadership positions and top key jobs in the organization. Help your people find their way to the path that's the best fit. Getting a good fit starts with an assessment of performance over time and an estimate of potential. Accurately make those assessments and provide people with the candid feedback that will help them realistically assess their career options. For general management roles, you need people high in learning agility. People who learn from experience. Who can transfer learning to new situations. People who can easily adapt. Change. Those qualities are not nearly as critical for most technical and professional roles. Research has shown that typical line managers have difficulty making tough calls on potential. Potential is not the same as performance. That's a mistake many managers make, and it decreases the accuracy of assessments. Teach your managers the difference and help them learn to accurately assess both performance and potential. This is important for career coaching, development, and support. Your talented professionals on a technical career path are different from those on a general management career path. They need to be treated differently. Developed differently. Supported differently.

☐ **4. Give managers the skills they need to provide career support.** It's not enough to select the best management candidates; you need to help them continuously grow and learn. Managers are a key link in the chain of career support. Devote at least as much energy to training the skills of managing and developing people as to technical skills training. Structure curricula around people management skills, like coaching and providing feedback. Studies show that training supervisors to give positive and constructive feedback improves their employees' job satisfaction and performance. The best managers are expert coaches. They have finely tuned listening skills. They have meaningful conversations that help employees understand what needs to be accomplished, how behaviors impact others, and what's possible to achieve in the future. In those conversations, they are present and focused on the employee. Not checking e-mail. Not glancing at their watch. They connect because they're truly interested and want the best for the employee and the organization. They raise self-awareness in others. They coach them in how to improve performance. They resolve conflicts, address them constructively and head-on. They ask questions that encourage involvement and promote a sense of ownership. They motivate, get others fired up to set and meet challenging goals. All these management behaviors benefit employees while engaging employees and driving organizational performance. Such behaviors should be taught and practiced in your management development programs. Incorporate role-play so managers practice coaching, practice having difficult conversations, and get lots of feedback from their peers. Ensure that managers are very knowledgeable about the key jobs, career paths, and the available career resources so they can readily answer questions and point employees in the right direction. Educate managers about the value of moving talent across organizational boundaries for development. Reward managers who promote their best talent as candidates for developmental assignments. Counsel those who resist and are protective of talent. Recognize and reward the managers who are most successful in developing talent and promoting movement through the talent pipeline.

☐ **5. Dedicate organizational resources to career development.** Career support is an important driver of employee engagement and warrants formal structure, staffing, and a budget. Formal structure means space, technology, and resources. Consider establishing a career center. Providing career counseling services. Establishing a library of related materials—books, articles, Web resources, overviews of the most significant jobs and career paths in the organization, a directory of career support services. Conduct career development seminars, Webinars, and brown bag lunch sessions that feature executives speaking about careers in the firm and outside experts speaking about general career development strategies. Partner with local educational institutions. Make career coaches available in the career center. Employees need to know they have a place to freely express their own career interests. A place where they will be listened to, will receive candid feedback on their requests, and are assured that legitimate actions will be taken on their behalf. Teach interviewing and selection techniques as a way to improve your hiring practices and also enable individuals to better assess and interview for internal positions. Encourage and prepare all managers to have meaningful career discussions, especially with motivated top performers. Talk is one thing. Resources are another. Things that are important get funding. Are you committing resources to build your employment brand? To creating career support collateral, Web sites, and development programs? There is a positive return on investments in career support.

☐ **6. Recognize and reward employee initiative.** The proverb gets it right: Give a person a fish and they will eat for a day. Teach a person to fish and they will eat for a lifetime. Empowerment is preferable to dependence. And that principle should guide your career support initiatives—design them to enable individuals to climb into the driver's seat and take control of their destiny. Promoting ownership and initiative is at the heart of a high-performance culture. Don't exempt career support from that focus. Drive it home by recognizing self-initiated development and individual career accomplishments. Highlight educational achievements in the employee newsletter, on the intranet, on the TV monitors in the cafeteria. Jane

Employee just received her MBA! Joe Employee just achieved his Project Management Professional Certification! Run personal interest stories that provide some personal details about the sacrifices individuals made to achieve their goals. Celebrate initiative. Celebrate great effort and hard work. Doing so will inspire others, will help drive a high-performance culture, and will positively impact employee engagement.

☐ **7. Establish progressive policies to enable career support.** How easy is it for your employees to find internal development opportunities? What's the application process? The approval process? What about for external development? How flexible is your tuition reimbursement program? Do you cover professional certifications? How about general education coursework that's not directly related to work? Are non-degree programs covered? What's the level of reimbursement? Explore ways to simplify and liberalize requirements. The more you do so, the more likely employees will avail themselves of internal and external development opportunities. Create an organizational mind-set that looks for ways to encourage development rather than restrict it. The idea is for employees to feel like the organization has paved the development road for them rather than constructed multiple barriers to overcome. And why not? If you're not confident that your employees are responsible adults who can be trusted to make good decisions and take charge of their development, it's a sign of deep-seated problems with your selection process and organizational culture. Do what it takes to solve those problems. Hire and promote responsible adults and revamp policies and procedures that place an unnecessary burden on them.

☐ **8. Develop talent strategically.** Align development and career support initiatives with your business strategy by addressing the gaps in your core leadership competencies, the competencies that will drive your strategy. Make those competencies the centerpiece of training and development in the organization. Develop instruction around the systems and processes created to optimize execution of your strategy. Teach analytical methods. Teach the business drivers for your organization. Teach problem-solving and decision-making techniques and involve employees in action-learning projects with real implications. Be realistic, though, about the limitations of training. Most competency gaps can only be partially addressed by training. People learn most of what they know by doing on the job and by working with others. Look to development activities such as special assignments to complete the picture. Design developmental opportunities to strengthen skills in strategy. Assign managers and key employees to organizational committees, task forces, and special projects for development. Employ action learning to get managers involved in solving real business problems while they collaborate and learn. Senior managers and board members should mentor, coach, and evaluate solutions created by project teams. Look for extracurricular learning activities that teach and reinforce strategic thinking—things such as serving on the board of a nonprofit or professional organization. And don't neglect the transfer of training back to the job. It's critical to ensure that what's learned in training and development is retained and applied on the job. Managers and supervisors must be involved in the transfer of training to make sure that people have opportunities to apply what they've learned and receive feedback on their performance.

☐ **9. Employ technology to remove friction from the career support process.** Explore how talent management software suites can empower managers and employees. These Web-based applications can support all phases of talent management: recruitment and selection, performance management and alignment, learning and development, compensation and total rewards, and deployment and succession. Studies have shown that organizations that use these tools have more effective talent management practices that translate into improved organizational performance. From the employees' perspective, it's liberating to be able to maintain personal profiles, view available positions in the organization, create and align performance goals, find and register for internal development opportunities, launch online learning applications, manage learning transcripts, apply for tuition reimbursement, and create development plans that support performance in current roles and prepare for future roles. Managers benefit, too, from the ability to track employee progress against performance and development goals, easily approve requests for development opportunities, manage merit pay budgets and make better compensation decisions, and be more effective in managing talent deployment and succession. Use the company intranet to complement the talent management application and reinforce your employment brand. Provide directories of career support services and related news items, highlight individual accomplishments, and provide messages from senior management that contribute to a high-performance learning culture. Technology is your friend. Embrace it. It can greatly enhance your career management efforts.

☐ **10. Establish key metrics for career development and act on measurement results.** There are any number of metrics to indicate the success of your career support efforts. It's important to choose a limited number of metrics that answer meaningful questions, are aligned with the business strategy, and—importantly—are actionable. What is the promotion rate? Average time to promotion? Retention rate? Voluntary turnover rate? Time to fill key positions? Diversity percentages in key positions? Development costs? Training transfer? Training impact? Satisfaction with development opportunities? Assess employee engagement related to career support. Select a validated, norm-referenced instrument that addresses the career support driver and has the capability to add a few of your own custom items. Measure engagement periodically, every two years at a minimum. Annually is better. Have outside consultants review and report on the data. Hold managers responsible for acting on engagement data related to career development. Assign a senior-level champion to each issue. Set goals and time frames. Share survey results and action plans with employees. Track progress closely and frequently. Note every movement of the needle. Follow up. Act. Communicate progress. Communicate successes.

> *People underestimate their capacity for change. There is never*
> *a right time to do a difficult thing. A leader's job is to*
> *help people have vision of their potential.*
> John Porter – Sociologist, professor, and writer

Suggested Readings

Arnold, J., & Davey, K. M. (1999). Graduates' work experiences as predictors of organisational commitment, intention to leave, and turnover: Which experiences really matter? *Applied Psychology: An International Review, 48,* 211-238.

Arthur, M. B., & Rousseau, D. M. (2001). *The boundaryless career: A new employment principle for a new organizational era.* NY: Oxford University Press.

Ashkenas, R., Ulrich, D., Jick, T., & Kerr, S. (1995). *The boundaryless organization: Breaking the chains of organizational structure.* San Francisco: Jossey-Bass.

Ball, B., & Jordan, M. (1997). An open-learning approach to career management and guidance. *British Journal of Guidance & Counseling, 25,* 507-517.

Baruch, Y., & Peiperl, M. (2000). Career management practices: An empirical survey and implications. *Human Resource Management, 39,* 347-366.

Branham, F. L. (2001). *Keeping the people who keep you in business: 24 Ways to hang on to your most valuable talent.* NY: AMACOM.

Brousseau, K. R., Driver, M. J., Eneroth, K., & Larsson, R. (1996). Career pandemonium: Realigning organizations and individuals. *Academy of Management Executive, 10,* 52-66.

Brown, D. (2007). *Career information, career counseling, and career development* (9th ed.). Needham Heights, MA: Allyn & Bacon.

Eby, L. T., Allen, T. D., & Brinley, A. (2005). A cross-level investigation of the relationship between career management practices and career-related attitudes. *Group & Organization Management, 30,* 565-596.

Eichinger, R. W., Lombardo, M. M., & Ulrich, D. (2004). *100 Things you need to know: Best people practices for managers & HR.* Minneapolis, MN: Lominger International: A Korn/Ferry Company.

Epperheimer, J. (1997). Benchmarking career management. *HR Focus, 74*(11), 9-10.

Feldman, D. C. (1988). *Managing careers in organizations.* Glenview, IL: Scott Foresman.

Feldman, D. C. (1995). The impact of downsizing on organizational career development activities and employee career development opportunities. *Human Resource Management Review, 5,* 189-221.

Greenhaus, J. H., Callanan, G. A., & Godshalk, V. M. (2000). Career management (3rd ed.). Fort Worth, TX: Dryden Press.

Gutteridge, T. G., & Otte, F. L. (1983). Organizational career development: What's going on out there? *Training and Development Journal, 37*(2), 22-26.

Joinson, C. (2001). Employee sculpt thyself...with a little help. *HR Magazine, 46*(5), 60-65.

Kaye, B. (2002). *Up is not the only way: A guide to developing workforce talent* (2nd ed.). Palo Alto, CA: Davies-Black.

Knowdell, R. L. (1996). *Building a career development program: Nine steps for effective implementation.* Palo Alto, CA: Davies-Black.

Kummerow, J. (2000). *New directions in career planning and the workplace* (2nd ed.). Palo Alto, CA: Davies-Black.

Lips-Wiersma, M., & Hall, D. T. (2007). Organizational career development is not dead: A case study on managing the new career during organizational change. *Journal of Organizational Behavior, 28,* 771-792.

Mallon, M., & Walton, S. (2005). Career and learning: The ins and the outs of it. *Personnel Review, 34,* 468-487.

McCall, M. W., Lombardo, M. M., & Morrison, A. M. (1988). *The lessons of experience: How successful executives develop on the job.* NY: Free Press.

Nelson, B. (1997). *1001 Ways to energize employees.* NY: Workman.

Niles, S. G., & Harris-Bowlsbey, J. (2004). *Career development interventions in the 21st century* (2nd ed.). Upper Saddle River, NJ: Prentice Hall.

Orpen, C. (1994). The effects of organizational and individual career management on career success. *International Journal of Manpower, 15,* 27-37.

Rothwell, W. J., Jackson, R. D., Knight, S. C., & Lindholm, J. E. (2005). *Career planning and succession management: Developing your organization's talent—for today and tomorrow.* Westport, CT: Praeger.

Sturges, J., Conway, N., Guest, D., & Liefooghe, A. (2005). Managing the career deal: The psychological contract as a framework for understanding career management, organizational commitment and work behavior. *Journal of Organizational Behavior, 26,* 821-838.

Sturges, J., Guest, D., Conway, N., & Davey, K. M. (2002). A longitudinal study of the relationship between career management and organizational commitment among graduates in the first ten years of work. *Journal of Organizational Behavior, 23,* 731-748.

Sullivan, S. E. (1999). The changing nature of careers: A review and research agenda. *Journal of Management, 25,* 457-484.

Van Maanen, J., & Schein, E. H. (1979). Toward a theory of organizational socialization. In B. M. Staw (Ed.), *Research in organizational behavior* (Vol. 1, pp. 206-264). Greenwich, CT: JAI.

Engagement Driver H
Nature of the Job

*I feel sorry for the person who can't get genuinely excited
about his work. Not only will he never be satisfied,
but he will never achieve anything worthwhile.*
Walter Chrysler – Automotive pioneer

The Signpost
Do your employees and available jobs fit well together? Do employees clearly understand expectations and receive regular feedback on performance. Do jobs provide opportunities for employees to use a variety of skills? Do employees feel their jobs are delivering something that's important to others? And do they have an appropriate level of independence to do their jobs? These are important considerations when designing jobs that engage.

Unskilled
- ☐ Is a poor judge of talent; assigns people to poor-fitting jobs
- ☐ Fails to clearly set expectations and communicate goals
- ☐ Doesn't provide training that's effective or sufficient to create confidence in skills
- ☐ Delegates ineffectively; too directive or fails to establish boundaries
- ☐ Fails to provide line of sight from jobs to full value chain and organization strategy
- ☐ Designs jobs poorly; tasks are too complex and ambiguous or too simple and boring
- ☐ Fails to provide employees the tools, materials, and guidance to do the job
- ☐ Avoids candid conversations with employees about their performance
- ☐ Ineffectively measures employee behavior and accomplishments
- ☐ Fails to solicit ideas and input from workforce about job design and process improvement
- ☐ Keeps people in jobs too long; doesn't promote cross-training and job rotation
- ☐ Implements unnecessarily restrictive policies and processes that stifle initiative

H

Skilled

- ☐ Accurately analyzes job requirements; effectively designs jobs that engage employees
- ☐ Clearly communicates organization strategy and explains the linkage to individual roles
- ☐ Clearly communicates expectations and performance goals
- ☐ Establishes effective measures of behavior and of accomplishments
- ☐ Actively solicits employee input; establishes channels and processes for collecting employee suggestions
- ☐ Acknowledges suggestions, provides feedback, and makes related decisions all in a timely manner
- ☐ Accurately assesses talent; is committed to finding and hiring the best fit for the job
- ☐ Coaches and mentors effectively; helps others learn from mistakes and failures
- ☐ Includes others in decision making, especially in decisions that impact their jobs
- ☐ Eliminates bureaucratic nonsense, policies and procedures that stifle initiative
- ☐ Delegates effectively; empowers employees within defined boundaries
- ☐ Passionately creates a culture of teamwork and trust

Some Causes

- ☐ Lack of listening and understanding what motivates workforce
- ☐ Unsophisticated organization and job design capabilities
- ☐ Lack of diversity and fresh perspectives
- ☐ Rigid; slow to adapt
- ☐ Micromanagement
- ☐ Poor delegation
- ☐ Conflict avoidance
- ☐ Insufficient resources devoted to development
- ☐ Inadequately developed team processes
- ☐ Lack of resources to support performance

H

The Ten Leadership Architect® Competencies Most Associated with This Engagement Driver *(in order of connectedness)*

56. Sizing Up People
18. Delegation
19. Developing Direct Reports and Others
20. Directing Others
33. Listening
65. *Managing* Vision and Purpose
12. Conflict Management
35. Managing and Measuring Work
36. Motivating Others
39. Organizing

The Map

Your employees likely spend more than half of their waking hours on the job. More time spent at work than with their spouse or significant other. More time with coworkers than with their children. More time doing the organization's bidding than pursuing personal interests. It's no surprise, then, that job design is a key driver of employee engagement. The nature of the job obviously impacts job satisfaction. But it also impacts key performance indicators for the business. Quality. Productivity. Customer service. Safety. Cost. Studies show that well-designed jobs reduce worker fatigue. They reduce levels of stress. Reduce boredom. Improve worker health. Well-designed jobs optimally challenge. Minimally frustrate. They can provide a sense of personal worth and meaning...or not. The design of the job will define your personnel selection criteria. Job design dictates the level of skills required for success. The level of education required. The background and experience needed. And for all those reasons, the nature of the jobs in your organization will significantly define your organizational culture. So, jobs are important. And job design requires a broad perspective, starting with the mission and strategic objectives of the business. Within that context, processes are engineered to serve the needs of internal and external customers. And each job spans some portion of those processes. In addition to strategic objectives and business processes, you've got to consider creation of supporting policies, identification of required skills, design of discrete tasks—the building blocks of primary job duties, requirements for tools and resources, application of ergonomic design principles, and compensation. It's a lot, to be sure. But when you've got it right, when you've selected the right individuals for well-designed jobs, everything fits. Jobs fit incumbents like a glove. Employees feel energized and empowered. They have just enough task variety to keep interested but not so much as to feel frenetic.

H

93

They have enough job-related information to successfully perform but not so much as to be overwhelmed. They possess enough skill to feel confident but not so much as to feel grossly underutilized. They have enough autonomy to feel independent but not so much as to feel isolated. They understand how their jobs provide value to the customer. How it fits in the big picture. In short, employees will be fully engaged. And for that, the organization benefits considerably.

Some Remedies

☐ **1. Implement a best-in-class performance management process.** A well-executed performance management process will do more to shape employee perceptions about their jobs than just about anything else you can do. The cornerstone of a well-executed process is the occurrence of frequent, meaningful conversations between the manager and employee. Those conversations provide clear communication about expectations and feedback on performance. And that information is a key to shaping perceptions about the job. Performance management involves goal setting, feedback and coaching, and assessment. When goals cascade from the top of the organization so all goals are aligned, it helps employees understand how their jobs fit into the big picture. It supports the notion that the job delivers value, provides something of importance to others. Performance management helps managers to connect the dots for their teams so no one in the organization is confused or ambivalent about their role. Beyond the impact on the nature of jobs, we know that a well-designed and administered performance management process drives organizational performance. Performance management aligns employee efforts with the strategic intent of the organization. It differentiates between levels of performance and helps create a high-performance culture. And, the research is crystal clear—people perform better when they have specific goals and when they receive feedback on their performance.

☐ **2. Search for opportunities to enlarge and enrich jobs.** Good job design ensures adequate task variety, imparts a sense of importance to the tasks performed, and provides an appropriate degree of autonomy. When jobs are too small or too mundane, employees disengage. Watch for signs of disengagement. Listen to employees. As soon as there is a sense that they need more challenge, more variety, more responsibility, begin to expand the job. Expanding the job doesn't necessarily mean rewriting the job description. Jobs can be enhanced by expanding horizontally—job enlargement. Or vertically—job enrichment. Job enlargement doesn't change the content of the job as much as it expands the scale. Adding direct reports. Taking responsibility for a larger sales territory. Adding

H

94

responsibility for marketing another product line. Taking on another major account. In all of these cases, the nature of the job changes little, but there is increased responsibility and challenge because of the growth in scale. Job enrichment does change the nature of the work. Enrichment adds new tasks and responsibilities that aren't part of the original job. Increasing decision-making authority. Adding accountability for new tasks. Assuming some of the management responsibility of the boss. In all of these cases, the nature of the job changes by virtue of additional planning, evaluation, organization, etc. Common methods for job enrichment include:

- *Combining serial or parallel tasks.* When tasks are combined, all tasks required to complete a given job are performed by one person rather than by a series of individuals who do separate, independent, small parts of the job. Combining tasks will increase skill variety and task identity.

- *Forming work into more natural units.* The parts of work handled by employees should be arranged into logical groupings. This will give employees continuing responsibility for an identifiable portion of work. For example, instead of assigning sales to one person and customer service to another, give sales and customer service responsibility for a particular geographic area to one person.

- *Assigning client relationship responsibility.* By enabling employees to manage clients, three core job dimensions are affected. Feedback increases because individuals have the opportunity to get direct praise and criticism for their work from clients. Skill variety increases because of the relating skills needed in maintaining good client relationships. Likewise, autonomy increases because workers have personal responsibility for deciding how to manage their own clients.

- *Increasing decision-making latitude.* Management sets objectives but gives the employee discretion to set schedules and determine work methods. Management defines what's to be accomplished, but the employee decides how to accomplish it.

- *Implementing job rotation.* Job enrichment can be achieved through job rotation—planned job swapping that requires learning new skills and performing new duties. In addition to adding task variety and providing development, job rotation can benefit the organization by creating a much more flexible workforce.

- *Assigning experts to mentoring and coaching roles.* Another way to enrich jobs for those who have achieved mastery level is to add coaching and mentoring responsibilities. This allows them to stay in

H

95

their role but gain additional variety and responsibility by sharing their expertise with others, another win-win situation for the employee and the organization.

☐ **3. Delegate effectively.** A primary job of management is to make sure that the jobs in the organization are designed well and defined clearly for employees. Effective delegation is a key part of that process. Effective delegation spells out the desired job outcomes—the accomplishments that define success. Effective delegation defines the boundaries within which employees do the job, exercise judgment, and have authority to make decisions. While it's important to clearly define desired outcomes, it's usually less important to define how the outcomes are achieved. Consider the capabilities of employees and provide only as much direction on how to achieve results as they need. Allow them to think, to be creative, to exercise discretion, to figure things out. To the extent possible, collaboratively set goals and schedules. Give them support as needed, but don't get in their way. Give them room to do the job. Minimize control and bureaucracy. Provide them with meaningful work, the tools and resources they need to be successful, and an enabling environment. If there are performance problems or there is a lack of engagement, the root cause is likely due to something in management's control. Management defines the nature of jobs. Management communicates requirements. Management provides tools and resources. And management is responsible for the work environment. If management is not attending to these things, it's failing.

☐ **4. Make good use of develop-in-place assignments.** There's a practical limit to how much jobs can be enhanced through enlargement and enrichment. Develop-in-place assignments don't change the job but do provide enrichment when employees take on some temporary additional responsibilities, typically without giving up much or any of their current responsibilities. These may be independent special projects. Investigate a recurring customer service issue and propose a solution. Assess several vendors competing for business and make a recommendation. Study an underperforming process and engineer an improvement. These are examples of one-off independent projects that provide task variety, offer an opportunity to learn new skills, and contribute meaningful value to the organization. Many develop-in-place assignments are team-based. Project teams, task forces, and other special team assignments also provide an excellent way for employees to develop new skills, obtain additional task variety, and experience a sense of accomplishment. In addition, the social interaction can be highly valued and have long-term benefits as networks are formed. When handpicked members from finance, engineering, marketing, and logistics get together to work as a cross-functional team on an important issue, great things can happen. In addition to the creative solutions that are often generated by the different perspectives, new relationships are formed. Team members get a greater understanding and appreciation of different parts of the organization. They learn how their individual and departmental performance affects others in the organization. Cross-functional teams and task forces provide a high-impact developmental experience. Members are forced to govern themselves, deal with ambiguous circumstances, plan, negotiate, navigate organizational politics, and sell their combined vision to the rest of the organization. The ability to influence without authority becomes critical. All of the skills learned can be transferred to other job situations in the future. All these benefits make a strong case for using cross-functional teams across the organization to solve enterprise-wide problems and enhance employee engagement.

☐ **5. Enhance your personnel selection criteria to achieve good fit with the job.** You can carefully design jobs to provide the right levels of information, feedback, task variety, task significance, and independence, but the question is: Right for whom? Even if you've attended to all the key factors when designing a job, you'll still have a disengaged employee if you do a poor job of selection when hiring. What constitutes meaningful information, task variety, job importance, and freedom differs from one person to another. You can err in either direction—by setting the selection bar too low or too high. Too low and you've got major problems on your hands—employees who, even if motivated, deliver poor performance and lack the capability of ever developing the skills the job requires. Too high and you'll soon have engagement issues because the intrinsic motivation isn't there. You've got great talent on the bus, but the ride is never going to please the overqualified employee unless you change the job to fit the employee. Put at least as much rigor into selecting the right employee as you do designing the job. That will result in the right work getting done in the right way by the right person. And the upshot will be better quality, better productivity, and a more engaged workforce.

☐ **6. Build confidence through effective learning and development.** Learning is acquiring the ability to do something new, something different. And humans are amazing learning machines. Learning starts by trying to reach a goal. We try. We fail. We change course. We learn. Throughout life we learn most of what we know by doing. It's no different on the job. We learn primarily by doing—or trying to do—the job. We make good efforts, sometimes fail, and continue to modify our behavior until we think we've got it right. Jobs teach us most of what we learn throughout our careers. After jobs, we learn the most from other people throughout our careers. If we observe others, we have an opportunity to learn. If we listen to others, we have an opportunity to learn. We can also learn by being formally instructed. Instruction is an experience thoughtfully designed to cause learning to occur. There are three necessary components to instruction—content, practice with feedback, and assessment. Providing effective workplace instruction to support certain tasks is not optional. It's essential. We simply can't afford to let people learn everything by making mistakes. Mistakes can be devastating and result in staggering costs, great damage, or serious injury. Effective workplace instruction contributes to improved productivity by reducing the time spent learning, by minimizing the time it takes to get employees performing at the desired levels. Effective workplace instruction results in a competent and confident employee. When employees are consciously competent, they thoroughly know the skills they need to be successful on the job—and they know that they know. They're confident in their ability because they've had practice with feedback and have had their skills formally assessed. And that confidence results in improved job satisfaction. The design of good instruction is a science. Use that science to create your workplace learning and development programs. Systematically apply established principles of instructional design and adult learning. It's not enough to teach the right stuff. You have to teach it in the right way. Don't do a one-way information dump and expect people to acquire new skills. Get learners involved and performing—practicing and receiving feedback. And don't neglect the transfer of training back to the job. It's critical to ensure that what's learned in training and development is retained and applied on the job. Managers and supervisors must be involved in the transfer of training to make sure that people have opportunities to apply what they've learned and receive feedback on their performance.

☐ **7. Provide tools, job aids, and supplies required by the job.** These are required by virtually all jobs. And when they're not readily available, frustration is rampant. Tools leverage physical capabilities. They make an employee faster. Stronger. Safer. They enable employees to measure, reach, adjust, etc. Pick an action verb. Almost any action performed on the job can be done more quickly, more accurately, and more safely when the appropriate tool is used. Make sure they're available and serviceable when employees need them. Job aids leverage cognitive abilities. They, in effect, make an employee smarter. Checklists. Decision tables. Flowcharts. Software applications. Anything that reduces reliance on memory, aids decisions, makes computations, etc. They're tools for the brain, and they're the stock-in-trade for almost all workers, and certainly for knowledge workers. Again, make sure they're available and serviceable when needed.

And don't neglect supplies—not just the mission-critical supplies, but the incidental items that are consumed during the course of a job. A painter with a pallet of paint buckets and a box full of paint brushers is still going to be frustrated if there are no stir sticks. It's ridiculous to provide knowledge workers with loads of technology but make them scrounge for decent pens and notepads. To prevent frustration, lost productivity, and disengagement, pay attention to the small stuff.

☐ **8. Support self-managed teams.** The nature of a job is greatly influenced by the amount of independence it affords, and that applies to independence for teams as well as individuals. Winning organizations know how to tap into the expertise of their people and how to leverage that expertise by bringing them together to work in self-managed work teams. Quality circles. Cross-functional teams. Action-learning assignments. Project teams set up to solve specific problems. There are plenty of opportunities. Look around for low-hanging fruit and tap the right individuals to serve in team roles. Don't get hung up on job titles, functions, or levels. In fact, the more diverse the team, the more diverse the thought process will likely be. Implement process engineering programs which empower people to continually reinvent more effective ways of doing business. Reduce organizational gridlock. Allow people to get obstacles out of the way so they can do their work better. It's a winning situation all around. The organization will benefit from a continuous flow of improvement and innovation. Employees will develop critical skills such as conflict management, problem solving, and business acumen. And their level of engagement will increase as they develop relationships and benefit from social interaction with coworkers. In turn, the organization benefits significantly.

☐ **9. Make collaborative goal setting the norm.** Research shows that highly engaged employees are goal oriented. And disengaged employees are often unclear about what's expected of them. Shared goals benefit the organization because they get everyone on the same page and pulling in the same direction. Efforts are coordinated and aligned. Goals provide clarity of purpose. Focus. They provide the basis for assessment of performance and enable more effective coaching. When managers collaborate with their employees to establish goals, they increase buy-in and motivation. Personal communication around goals fosters ownership and understanding. It's an opportunity to help employees understand how their accomplishments make a difference and fit in the big picture. When employees have a sense of personal accountability for achieving goals, engagement increases. Urge managers to collaborate with employees in one-on-one meetings to define, review, and revise goals. Generally, people perform better with goals that can be realistically reached by putting forth significant effort. Stretch goals are especially helpful in pushing for new skills. Research shows that when goals are set appropriately and communicated clearly, there is a more favorable perception of the job and increased engagement.

☐ **10. Build a feedback-rich environment.** The amount and quality of feedback is a key component of any job. At the outset of the supervisor-employee relationship, establish a high-candor-feedback protocol. Managers should explain that the purpose of feedback is to help guide and support the employee to be successful in the job. In addition to setting the expectation that the employee will regularly receive candid feedback, the manager should ask for regular feedback from the employee. Establishing expectations around feedback in this way communicates positive intent and helps remove tension. In organizations that have created a culture steeped in candor and straight talk, giving and receiving feedback is as natural as breathing. Feedback is given frequently, usually in real time during and immediately following performance. The feedback is tied to goals. Performance goals. Developmental goals. Career goals. Feedback on performance helps employees adjust what they are doing along the way and make midcourse corrections. Developmental and career feedback shows employees that what they are doing is important and that the manager is there to help them grow and progress with the organization. Encourage managers to view giving—and receiving—feedback as a gift, not a burden. Start a campaign. Begin at the top. A campaign to give more candid and critical feedback. Require performance evaluation grades to be distributed or rank ordered. Require managers to spread out their ratings. Make sure feedback is balanced with as much critical and constructive feedback as positive. Use 360° techniques. Anonymous feedback tends to be more accurate than face-to-face. Make your environment a feedback-rich environment, and supplement the feedback with coaching and mentoring to encourage and guide development in the core competencies.

My first six years in the business were hopeless. There are
a lot of times when you sit and you say 'Why am I doing this?
I'll never make it. It's just not going to happen.
I should go out and get a real job and try to survive.'
George Lucas – Filmmaker, creator of Star Wars
and Indiana Jones franchises

H

Suggested Readings

Brannick, M. T., Levine, E. L., & Morgeson, F. P. (2007). *Job and work analysis: Methods, research, and applications for human resource management.* Thousand Oaks, CA: Sage.

Burr, R., & Cordery, J. L. (2001). Self-management efficacy as a mediator of the relation between job design and employee motivation. *Human Performance, 14,* 27-44.

Burton, R. M., De Sanctis, G., & Obel, B. (2006). *Organizational design: A step-by-step approach.* NY: Cambridge University Press.

Galbraith, J. R. (2002). *Designing organizations: An executive guide to strategy, structure, and process.* San Francisco: Jossey-Bass.

Galbraith, J. R., Downey, D., & Kates, A. (2002). *Designing dynamic organizations: A hands-on guide for leaders at all levels.* NY: AMACOM.

Gallos, J. V. (Ed.). (2006). *Organization development: A Jossey-Bass reader.* San Francisco: Jossey-Bass.

Hackman, J., & Oldham, R. (1976). Motivation through the design of work: Test of a theory. *Organizational Behavior & Human Performance, 16,* 250-279.

Jones, G. R. (2006). *Organizational theory, design and change* (5th ed.). Upper Saddle River, NJ: Prentice Hall.

Kabachnick, T. (2006). *I quit, but forgot to tell you.* Largo, FL: Kabachnick Group.

Karasek, R. A. (1979). Job demands, job decision latitude, and mental strain: Implications for job redesign. *Administrative Science Quarterly, 24,* 285-309.

Kates, A., & Galbraith, J. R. (2007). *Designing your organization: Using the STAR model to solve 5 critical design challenges.* San Francisco: Jossey-Bass.

Konrad, A. M. (2006). Engaging employees through high-involvement work practices. *Ivey Business Journal, 70*(4), 1-6.

Lencioni, P. M. (2007). *The three signs of a miserable job: A fable for managers (and their employees).* San Francisco: Jossey-Bass.

May, D. R., Gilson, R. L., & Harter, L. M. (2004). The psychological conditions of meaningfulness, safety and availability and the engagement of the human spirit at work. *Journal of Occupational & Organizational Psychology, 77,* 11-37.

McCauley, C. D. (2006). *Developmental assignments: Creating learning experiences without changing jobs.* Greensboro, NC: Center for Creative Leadership.

McShane, S. L., & Von Glinow, M. A. (2008). *Organizational behavior: Emerging realities for the workplace revolution* (4th ed.). NY: McGraw-Hill/Irwin.

Nelson, B. (1997). *1001 Ways to energize employees.* NY: Workman.

Parker, S. K., & Wall, T. D. (1998). *Job and work design: Organizing work to promote well-being and effectiveness.* Thousand Oaks, CA: Sage.

Salendy, G. (Ed.). (2006). *Handbook of human factors and ergonomics* (3rd ed.). Hoboken, NJ: John Wiley & Sons.

H

Sirota, D., Mischkind, L. A., & Meltzer, M. I. (2005). *The enthusiastic employee: How companies profit by giving workers what they want.* Upper Saddle River, NJ: Pearson Education.

Towers Perrin. (2003). *The 2003 Towers Perrin Talent Report: Working today: Understanding what drives employee engagement.* Retrieved January 15, 2009, from http://www.towersperrin.com/tp/getwebcachedoc?webc=HRS/USA/2003/200309/Talent_2003.pdf

Wallgren, L. G., & Hanse, J. J. (2006). Job characteristics, motivators, and stress among information technology consultants: A structural equation modeling approach. *International Journal of Industrial Ergonomics, 37,* 51-59.

Engagement Driver 1
Developmental Opportunities

We learn geology the morning after the earthquake.
Ralph Waldo Emerson – Philosopher and poet

The Signpost
If you're not providing opportunities for your employees to learn and grow, they'll go someplace else, to another organization that will provide those opportunities. Management ranks are typically rife with misconceptions about how people develop. How will you help your managers learn to analyze developmental needs? To effectively prescribe training and development solutions? To ensure that learning is transferred from coursework to the job? Answer these questions or risk disengagement of your key employees.

Unskilled
- ☐ Deploys talent without considering development opportunities; solely considers operational needs of the business
- ☐ Invests insufficient resources in developmental programs
- ☐ Is swayed by fads when selecting training content; fails to strategically align with business
- ☐ Provides limited or no financial support for continuing education and development
- ☐ Designs training poorly; fails to effectively build skills and impart confidence
- ☐ Punishes risk takers and well-intentioned nonconformists
- ☐ Holds talented people in jobs for too long
- ☐ Is ineffective in providing feedback and coaching
- ☐ Fails to implement develop-in-place assignments
- ☐ Doesn't hold managers accountable for development of their people
- ☐ Is organized with silos and roadblocks that stifle learning
- ☐ Doesn't study failures; repeats mistakes

Skilled
- ☐ Effectively assesses skills provided by jobs; uses information for developmental assignments
- ☐ Provides ample mix of developmental opportunities through jobs, training, coaching, and develop-in-place assignments

- ☐ Celebrates creativity and risk taking; understands failures are part of learning
- ☐ Coaches and mentors effectively; helps others learn from mistakes and failures
- ☐ Ties executive and manager incentives to development of staff
- ☐ Invests significant executive and management time in the development of others
- ☐ Makes tuition reimbursement and other financial support programs widely available across the organization
- ☐ Finds ways to accommodate employees' needs to take time out for development
- ☐ Develops high-quality training programs that are aligned with strategic needs and adult learning principles
- ☐ Passionately creates an organizational culture of continuous learning
- ☐ Accurately appraises performance and potential; matches developmental assignments with individual needs
- ☐ Relentlessly identifies and removes organizational barriers, policies and practices that hinder development

Some Causes

- ☐ Lack of resources to support development
- ☐ Inadequate development of people strategy
- ☐ Narrow perspective; short-term view
- ☐ Organizational barriers, silos
- ☐ Inability to accurately size up people
- ☐ Failure to discriminate performance levels and treat people differently
- ☐ Senior management not engaged in talent process
- ☐ Unrealistic expectations for training results
- ☐ Complacency
- ☐ Procrastination

The Ten Leadership Architect® Competencies Most Associated with This Engagement Driver *(in order of connectedness)*

19. Developing Direct Reports and Others
12. Conflict Management
18. Delegation
46. Perspective
13. Confronting Direct Reports
 2. *Dealing with* Ambiguity

41. Patience
56. Sizing Up People
62. Time Management
33. Listening

The Map

Employee learning and development: Many organizations simply don't get it. Of all the major talent management functions, employee learning and development is perhaps the most likely to lack sophistication. Research shows that strategic investments in the development of human capital provide a significant financial return through gains in productivity, employee retention, and market capitalization. But many organizations apparently don't get it. They under-invest in lean times and over-invest aimlessly when times are good. Many organizations fail to invest strategically. They spread resources like butter on bread across a broad portfolio of training programs that, for the most part, don't impact the right employees and the roles that most matter. They ignore the 70:20:10 rule of thumb—70% of learning comes from the job, 20% from others, and just 10% from courses. They adopt silly policies that, for instance, require every employee to spend a minimum number of hours in traditional training programs. Jane gets 80 hours. Joe gets 80 hours. That Jane and Joe are in very different roles and have starkly different development needs doesn't matter. It's 80 hours for everyone. The widespread lack of sophistication restricts the organizational view of development to traditional training instructor-led courses, e-learning courses, seminars, workshops—all programs that have well-defined learning objectives, a content outline, and a defined time frame—everything tied up neatly with a bow. Truth is, the most effective learning experiences are often messy and occur on the job. We learn by doing and by failing. We learn from watching and listening to others. That's not to say, of course, that traditional training programs are unimportant. If done right, they address vital strategic business needs. They create a competitive edge. They engage the workforce. If done right, they build skills that differentiate your organization. They provide significant practice and meaningful feedback. They incorporate assessment. They don't end at 5 p.m. on Friday afternoon. If done right, the learning continues and is transferred to the job under the watchful eye of the boss, who makes sure that skills continue to be practiced and assessed. That's strategic training. Training that benefits employees and drives organizational performance. Development that drives employee engagement.

Some Remedies

☐ **1. Establish a learning culture.** Learning is acquiring the ability to do something new, something different. Learning organizations adapt. They create knowledge, organize it, share it, and protect it. They are learning agile. They tolerate, even celebrate, mistakes because they treat them as opportunities for learning. They have embedded knowledge management into their systems and they embrace change. This is a profitable path to business success. Promote organizational learning with a passion. Provide mechanisms for sharing learning across groups. Set up communities of practice. Find ways to centralize information so that it can be easily accessed throughout the organization. Use action-learning assignments to simultaneously stretch people and solve organizational problems. Create a shared mind-set about learning that includes a commitment to openness, to listening. The shared mind-set is best set collectively through open dialog and problem solving. It needs to be well communicated and translated into day-to-day behaviors. Weave the necessity for and willingness to learn into the fabric of the enterprise. Clear the collective-thinking stream of biases, unsupported assumptions, prejudices, preconceived conclusions, and inappropriate advocacy. Work on the nature of the thinking and decision-making processes in the organization so that they are free of personalized arguments and power-based preferences. Ensure that thinking and decision-making processes don't default to those in power. Give everyone feedback about their behavior in decision-making settings. Teach appreciative inquiry—a focus on improving what's already working rather than a focus on what's not working. Have a real commitment to the unvarnished truth. It is much easier to have a learning organization if you have leaders who model active learning. Some research has shown that as leaders move to the top, they actually listen less and depend upon themselves more. Turn that on its head so that the leaders at the top are the model listeners and learners in the organization. Institutionalize the practice of postmortem meetings and other processes to capture lessons learned. Never leave an event or complete a project—good or bad— without debriefing what worked and what didn't. Learn from successes and failure. Carry the learnings forward to apply to future situations. Live and breathe organizational learning.

☐ **2. Use a job assignment strategy to get the most mileage out of development.** The old saying is true—experience really is the best teacher. Research strongly supports the conventional wisdom that people learn by doing. Yet when it comes to development planning, the emphasis is often put on formal training courses as the means to build skills. It turns out that formal training and coursework account for only a small percentage, around 10%, of the learning managers and executives need to develop mission-critical skills. The short answer for how people best develop skills is jobs. About 70% of a person's development happens through challenging and, in many cases, first-time job assignments. The valuable lessons a person learns typically happen in jobs that force them to move out of their comfort zone. There needs to be something at stake, where success or failure depends on their ability to learn something new. Repetition of skills is not the same as development. For a job to be developmental, it has to be more than just a straight-line promotion. It is not enough for the job to be "new"; it has to be an assignment where the learner does not have all the necessary tools at the outset. Instead, they must stretch their current skill set and expend a lot of effort in order to succeed. Some jobs have more developmental horsepower. Jobs that are high impact. High risk. And, as a result, provide great opportunities for learning. Like managing a major change initiative. Turning around a failing business. Or starting a brand-new one. Taking a global assignment. Build a job assignment system into your overall development strategy. Only by using the company as the classroom, can average employees become extraordinary ones.

☐ **3. Use action learning to turn the company into a classroom.** Action learning is a teaching method that assigns a real-world problem for a group of learners to solve. To be effective, action-learning assignments should represent a valid and significant business problem or opportunity. The stakes should be high. The problems should present a difficult challenge for the group. Typically, the assignments are part of a learning experience that spans quite a bit of time, usually several weeks or months. The group is given resources and time to analyze the problem/opportunity, develop and test alternate approaches, and select and implement a solution. The possibility of failure is real, and since the team's success is typically reviewed several management levels up in the organization, there is a lot of pressure to succeed. Action learning is a high-impact method that is especially appropriate for leadership and management development programs. It benefits the organization by stretching learners to gain new skills and by delivering solutions with real value to the business.

☐ **4. Search for development opportunities outside the organization.** Organizational committees, task forces, and special projects can be very effective development assignments, especially for managers and key employees. Those opportunities can sometimes be in short supply inside the organization, but there are usually many similar opportunities outside the organization. Look to local community groups, nonprofit organizations, and professional associations for development opportunities. These roles can be identified as part of a formal individual development plan with defined objectives and regular progress reporting to the manager. Extracurricular learning activities such as serving on the board of a nonprofit or professional organization can teach and reinforce strategic thinking and other skills required at senior levels. Remember that the best developmental opportunities involve risk. Comfort is the enemy of growth and development, so counsel people to move outside of their comfort zone. To make real development happen, encourage employees to look for development opportunities that go against their grain, even when going outside the organization.

☐ **5. Require the organization and individual to share financial and time burdens.** How easy is it for your employees to find internal development opportunities? What's the application process? The approval process? What about for external development? How flexible is your tuition reimbursement program? Do you cover professional certifications? How about general education coursework that's not directly related to work? Are non-degree programs covered? What's the level of reimbursement? Explore ways to simplify and liberalize requirements. The more you do so, the more likely employees will avail themselves of internal and external development opportunities. Create an organizational mind-set that looks for ways to encourage development rather than restrict it. The idea is for employees to feel like the organization has paved the development road for them rather than constructed multiple barriers to overcome. And why not? If you're not confident that your employees are responsible adults who can be trusted to make good decisions and take charge of their development, it's a sign of deep-seated problems with your selection processes and organizational culture. Do what it takes to solve those problems. Hire and promote responsible adults and revamp policies and procedures that place an unnecessary burden on them. That doesn't mean that employees won't make a sacrifice, too. And that's the ideal situation. Shared responsibility. Both parties have skin in the game. The organization has policies in place that provide a high level of visible support for self-directed development. At the same time, the employee expends time, energy, and in many cases, out-of-pocket payments for that part of tuition that is not covered by the organization. Studies indicate that engagement is higher and turnover is lower when such programs are in place.

☐ **6. Make sure learning transfers to the job.** If the learning experience is well designed and managed, learning will occur. But that doesn't necessarily mean the learning will be applied on the job. The main impediments to transfer include lack of manager involvement, lack of opportunities for application, lack of feedback on performance, and lack of reinforcement. Research suggests that the single biggest factor influencing learning transfer is the involvement of the immediate manager. Get the learner's manager involved before the program begins. Ideally, the learner and manager both agree to a learning contract which defines the learning objectives and outlines how learning will be applied on the job. Management involvement prior to the start of the program is a motivator for learners and helps get learning started on the right foot. After the learning experience, it's absolutely essential that the skills learned are regularly practiced until they're truly internalized. The manager should make sure those opportunities are available and should monitor progress and provide frequent feedback and coaching around the performance of skills that were learned. The manager is also responsible for providing positive reinforcement. Surveys of training professionals indicate that the percentage of what's learned that is actually transferred to the job is abysmally low. If a learning program is worthy of an investment for development and delivery, it's certainly worthy of the effort to ensure learning transfer.

☐ **7. Build a feedback-rich culture.** Great development doesn't just happen. It requires motivated learners who have opportunities to perform new skills and receive timely and actionable feedback on their performance. Establish direct, candid feedback as a pillar of your organizational culture. Institutionalize feedback as a key component of the supervisor-employee relationship. Managers should explain that the purpose of feedback is to help guide and support the employee to be successful in the job. In addition to setting the expectation that the employee will regularly receive candid feedback, the manager should ask for regular feedback from the employee. Establishing expectations around feedback in this way communicates positive intent and helps remove tension. In organizations that have created a culture steeped in candor and straight talk, giving and receiving feedback is as natural as breathing. Feedback is given frequently, usually in real time during or immediately following performance. The feedback is tied to goals. Performance goals. Developmental goals. Career goals. Feedback on performance helps employees adjust what they are doing along the way and make midcourse corrections. Developmental and career feedback shows employees that what they are doing is important and that the manager is there to help them grow and progress with the organization. People and organizations can't learn without it. Infuse your culture with feedback.

☐ **8. Create a culture that promotes calculated risk taking.** Playing it safe is not a path to learning and development. Neither is being reckless. Find the balance that promotes calculated risk taking. Develop methods for risk analysis and to define risk thresholds based on the impact of the decision, good or bad. Teach employees to assess risks and how to set confidence levels that are factored into decisions. It takes a certain amount of management humility to listen and be receptive to ideas from the rank and file, to allow them to participate in decisions. It takes management restraint to turn loose, to give up control and allow employees to pursue risky initiatives. And it takes a certain amount of management selflessness to give credit and recognize others. Management humility, restraint, and selflessness are hallmarks of participative, innovative, and risk-taking cultures. The cultures that contribute to accelerated learning and development. The cultures that lead to high levels of employee engagement. Publicly support employee decisions that are well-thought-out and stand behind employees as they try new things. Nothing stifles initiative more than continually being second-guessed. Recognize people who take appropriate risks. Recognize valiant attempts that end in failure. Send a clear message that there is amnesty for reasonable, calculated risks that don't pan out. Sometimes the greatest leaps forward in innovation come from learning what *not* to do. So treat the organization like a classroom and involve everyone in continuous learning.

☐ **9. Develop talent strategically.** There are several problems inherent in traditional training programs. Training is expensive. It's difficult to schedule. Learning is temporary unless the learner has adequate opportunities to use what's learned back on the job. And it's itinerant—learning moves with the person, even when the learner leaves your organization. Inherent problems, yes. Does that mean you should then abandon learning and development investments? No! If you abandon development, you'll be forced into continually recruiting new talent to meet your internal needs for key skills. And what happens in the likely event that your strategy points to a unique combination of skills not readily available in the labor market? No, don't abandon learning and development. Do it strategically and do it well. Align learning and development initiatives with your business strategy by addressing the gaps in your core leadership competencies— the competencies that drive your strategy. Make those competencies the centerpiece of training and development in the organization. Develop instruction around the systems and processes created to optimize execution of your strategy. Teach analytical methods. Teach the business drivers for your organization. Teach problem-solving and decision-making techniques and involve employees in action-learning projects with real implications. Be realistic, though, about the limitations of training. Most competency gaps can only be partially addressed by training. People learn most of what they know by doing on the job and by working with others. Look to development activities such as special assignments to complete the picture. Senior managers and board members should mentor, coach, and evaluate solutions created by project teams. Avoid a one-size-fits-all approach to development. Customize development based on the needs of employees and their placement in key roles. For general management roles, you need people high in learning agility. People who learn from experience. Who can transfer learning to new situations. People who can easily adapt. Change. Those qualities are not nearly as critical for most technical and professional roles. Potential is not the same as performance. Teach your managers the difference and help them learn to accurately assess both performance and potential. This is important so you can customize your treatment of talent. Your talented professionals on a technical career path are different than those on a general management career path. They need to be treated differently. Developed differently.

☐ **10. Design effective learning experiences.** Studies show that job-related learning primarily occurs by doing the job and secondarily occurs by interacting with and observing others on the job. Traditional classroom instruction typically provides the least amount of job-related learning, but that doesn't mean it's not important. Well-designed training can help people start a job higher on the learning curve and can accelerate their climb from that advanced starting point. So, what is well-designed training? In many instances, it's an experience that closely mirrors the experience of the job. That experience includes content focused on facts, concepts, and principles required on the job. There is plenty of opportunity for practice and feedback. You can think about the practice component as a simulation of the performance required by the job. High-fidelity simulations closely match the performance required on the job and create very effective learning activities. In addition to content and practice, there is assessment. You need all three—content, practice, and assessment. There is a well-established science of instructional design and a well-documented body of knowledge about adult learning principles. Implement best practices from these disciplines when designing learning experiences. When you do, you'll likely have motivated learners participating in highly interactive learning experiences that can easily transfer to the job. Evaluation should be ongoing throughout the design, delivery, and postdelivery follow-through of learning and development programs. Formative evaluation occurs on the fly during the development of instruction. Use formative evaluation to ensure that content and methods will effectively meet the performance objectives. Confirm the integrity of the design by performing frequent assessments of program components as they're being developed—expert reviews for content validity, usability testing, alpha testing of learning activities, instructional materials review, etc. Doing so will give you confidence the program will achieve its goals and be well received right out of the chute. There are also several levels of summative evaluation that can and should be employed after the program is implemented. At a minimum, evaluate the program by getting learner reactions to determine what worked well and what can be improved. Identify organizational performance metrics that are affected by the program and monitor the impact on business results. Use care to identify metrics in which the cause-and-effect relationship is clear. While it's important to evaluate program effectiveness, it's absolutely essential to assess the learner's performance. Do this periodically during the instruction as progress checks to ensure that learners are mastering skills, and again at the end of the program to assess overall mastery. To measure the transfer of learning to the job, assess performance yet again at a reasonable point in the future. Three months, six months—whatever time span is appropriate to ensure that learners have had opportunity to apply their new skills. This assessment can take several forms—skill checks, review of documented work performance, or supervisor ratings, for instance. Investments in learning and development are significant and deserve to be evaluated with the same rigor used by the business to evaluate other investments.

The more you develop people, the greater will be your confidence in them
when you thrust bigger and bigger jobs upon them.
Dwight D. Eisenhower – General of the Army and U.S. President

Suggested Readings

Bassi, L. J., & McMurrer, D. (2004). How's your return on people? *Harvard Business Review, 82*(3), 18.

Bassi, L. J., & McMurrer, D. (2007). Maximizing your return on people. *Harvard Business Review, 85*(3), 115-123.

Bassi, L. J., & Van Buren, M. E. (1999). Valuing investments in intellectual capital. *International Journal of Technology Management, 18*, 414-432.

Branham, F. L. (2001). *Keeping the people who keep you in business: 24 Ways to hang on to your most valuable talent.* NY: AMACOM.

Branham, F. L. (2005). *The 7 hidden reasons employees leave: How to recognize the subtle signs and act before it's too late.* NY: AMACOM.

Broad, M. L. (2005). *Beyond transfer of training: Engaging systems to improve performance.* San Francisco: Pfeiffer.

Broad, M. L., & Newstrom, J. W. (1992). *Transfer of training: Action-packed strategies to ensure high payoff from training investments.* Cambridge, MA: Perseus Books Group.

Brousseau, K. R., Driver, M. J., Eneroth, K., & Larsson, R. (1996). Career pandemonium: Realigning organizations and individuals. *Academy of Management Executive, 10*, 52-66.

Capelli, P. (2008). *Rethinking employee development.* Retrieved January 15, 2009, from http://www.hreonline.com/HRE/printstory.jsp?storyId=90138057

Charan, R. (2007). *Know-how: The 8 skills that separate people who perform from those who don't.* NY: Crown Business.

Chawla, S., & Renesch, J. (Eds.). (2006). *Learning organizations: Developing cultures for tomorrow's workplace.* Portland, OR: Productivity Press.

Cohen, D., & Prusak, L. (2001). *In good company: How social capital makes organizations work.* Boston, MA: Harvard Business School Press.

Dotlich, D. L., & Noel, J. L. (1998). *Action learning: How the world's top companies are re-creating their leaders and themselves.* San Francisco: Jossey-Bass.

Eichinger, R. W., Lombardo, M. M., & Stiber, A. (2006). *Broadband talent management: Paths to improvement.* Minneapolis, MN: Lominger International: A Korn/Ferry Company.

Eichinger, R. W., Lombardo, M. M., & Ulrich, D. (2004). *100 Things you need to know: Best people practices for managers & HR.* Minneapolis, MN: Lominger International: A Korn/Ferry Company.

Gagne, R. M., Wager, W. W, Golas, K., & Keller, J. M. (2005). *Principles of instructional design* (5th ed.). Belmont, CA: Wadsworth.

Goldsmith, M., & Reiter, M. (2007). *What got you here won't get you there: How successful people become even more successful.* NY: Hyperion.

Joinson, C. (2001). Employee sculpt thyself...with a little help. *HR Magazine, 46*(5), 60-65.

Kaye, B. (2002). *Up is not the only way: A guide to developing workforce talent* (2nd ed.). Palo Alto, CA: Davies-Black Publishing.

Kirkpatrick, D. L., & Kirkpatrick, J. D. (2005). *Transferring learning to behavior: Using the four levels to improve performance.* San Francisco: Berrett-Koehler.

Mager, R. F. (1999). *What every manager should know about training: An insider's guide to getting your money's worth from training.* Atlanta, GA: CEP Press.

Mallon, M., & Walton, S. (2005). Career and learning: The ins and the outs of it. *Personnel Review, 34,* 468-487.

Marquardt, M. J. (1999). *Action learning in action: Transforming problems and people for world-class organizational learning.* Palo Alto, CA: Davies-Black.

Marquardt, M. J. (2002). *Building the learning organization* (2nd ed.). Mountain View, CA: Davies-Black.

Marquardt, M. J. (2004). *Optimizing the power of action learning: Solving problems and building leaders in real time.* Palo Alto, CA: Davies-Black.

McCall, M. W., Lombardo, M. M., & Morrison, A. M. (1988). *The lessons of experience: How successful executives develop on the job.* NY: Free Press.

O'Neil, J., & Marsick, V. J. (2007). *Understanding action learning.* NY: American Management Association.

Rothwell, W. J. (1999). *The action learning guidebook: A real-time strategy for problem solving, training design, and employee development.* San Francisco: Jossey-Bass.

Rothwell, W. J., Jackson, R. D., Knight, S. C., & Lindholm, J. E. (2005). *Career planning and succession management: Developing your organization's talent—for today and tomorrow.* Westport, CT: Praeger.

Seijts, G. H., & Crim, D. (2006). What engages employees the most or, the ten C's of employee engagement. *Ivey Business Journal, 70,* 1-5.

Senge, P. M. (2006). *The fifth discipline: The art & practice of the learning organization.* NY: Doubleday Currency.

Silberman, M. L. (2005). *101 Ways to make training active.* San Francisco: Pfeiffer.

Stolovitch, H. (2002). *Telling ain't training.* Alexandria, VA: American Society for Training and Development.

Stolovitch, H. (2004). *Training ain't performance.* Alexandria, VA: American Society for Training and Development.

Ulrich, D., Eichinger, R. W., Kulas, J. T., & De Meuse, K. P. (2007). *50 More things you need to know: The science behind best people practices for managers & HR professionals.* Minneapolis, MN: Lominger International: A Korn/Ferry Company.

Ulrich, D., & Smallwood, N. (2003). *How leaders build value: Using people, organization, and other intangibles to get bottom-line results.* Hoboken, NJ: John Wiley & Sons.

Van Adelsberg, D., & Trolley, E. A. (1999). *Running training like a business: Delivering unmistakable value.* San Francisco: Berrett-Koehler Publishers.

Wick, C. (1996). *The learning edge.* NY: McGraw-Hill.

Wick, C., Pollock, R., Jefferson, A., Flanagan, R., & Wilde, K. (2006). *The six disciplines of breakthrough learning: How to turn training and development into business results.* San Francisco: Pfeiffer.

Engagement Driver J
Employee Recognition

I praise loudly, I blame softly.
Catherine the Great – Empress of Russia

The Signpost
Simple verbal recognition for a job well done is easy to provide and costs nothing. And it's one of the most powerful motivational tools at a manager's disposal. Research studies have consistently shown that providing employee recognition improves morale, commitment, and retention. It significantly improves employee engagement. Acknowledgement of employee contribution is not a sign of managerial softness and doesn't take much time. Conversely, and more to the point, it is a direct indicator of management's focus on performance.

Unskilled
- ☐ Doesn't plan or budget for formal recognition
- ☐ Fails to align recognition initiatives with business goals and organizational culture
- ☐ Doesn't clearly communicate expectations and goals
- ☐ Doesn't use appropriate timing in delivering recognition and reinforcement
- ☐ Relies solely on tangible incentives to provide motivation; doesn't fully understand or utilize intangible rewards and recognition
- ☐ Fails to understand workforce motivators; does not personalize recognition
- ☐ Focuses on minimum performance rather than optimum
- ☐ Does not establish effective measures of behavior and of accomplishments
- ☐ Avoids candid conversations with employees about their performance
- ☐ Unwilling or unable to discriminate between high and low performers
- ☐ Does not provide recognition equitably; plays favorites
- ☐ Makes clumsy and ineffective presentations for employee recognition

115

Skilled

- ☐ Creates a culture of open communication and appreciation
- ☐ Develops a comprehensive recognition strategy that includes formal and informal methods for recognizing employee contribution
- ☐ Establishes baseline measures of recognition; regularly monitors and makes adjustments
- ☐ Budgets adequately for recognition
- ☐ Understands what types of recognition are meaningful for groups and individuals; provides personalized reinforcement and recognition
- ☐ Aligns recognition initiatives with organizational strategy and culture
- ☐ Designs recognition programs that are simple to administer
- ☐ Administers formal recognition consistently, fairly, and in a timely manner across the organization
- ☐ Equips managers with interpersonal and coaching skills needed to provide meaningful feedback
- ☐ Effectively celebrates accomplishments with employees
- ☐ Recognizes and reinforces incremental improvements in performance
- ☐ Explains how individual performance impacts the team and the organization

Some Causes

- ☐ Lack of managerial courage
- ☐ Failure to discriminate performance levels and treat people differently
- ☐ Conflict avoidance
- ☐ Lack of listening and understanding what motivates workforce
- ☐ Tolerance for mediocrity
- ☐ Low levels of trust
- ☐ Poor time management
- ☐ Lack of creativity
- ☐ Inadequate planning
- ☐ Intolerant of diversity

The Ten Leadership Architect® Competencies Most Associated with This Engagement Driver *(in order of connectedness)*

35. Managing and Measuring Work
56. Sizing Up People
12. Conflict Management
13. Confronting Direct Reports
23. Fairness to Direct Reports

36. Motivating Others
65. *Managing* Vision and Purpose
 2. *Dealing with* Ambiguity
17. Decision Quality
52. Process Management

The Map

Recognition. Appreciation. Just simple acknowledgement. Everyone wants it. Everyone needs it. So why are we so stingy with it? It's a striking paradox. Why should it be so difficult to recognize a job well done? To let employees know that their contributions matter? Studies by the U.S. Department of Labor suggest that 64% of workers leave their jobs because they don't feel appreciated. Yet in many organizations, it's done poorly and infrequently. In fact, research by Gallup and other organizations indicates that up to 70% of employees report that they receive no recognition on the job from their boss. None! But some organizations do understand the power of the employee-recognition lever. They put resources toward recognition. They design formal recognition programs that are simple to administer and they execute them consistently and fairly. They have a variety of techniques and formats for delivering recognition. Managers personally express appreciation. Managers write notes to recognize good performance. Managers publicly provide recognition for outstanding performers. And managers organize ceremonies and parties to recognize team success. Those managers are equipped by the organization with skills and techniques that allow them to deliver individualized, informal recognition in a sincere and timely manner. They have conversations. Many conversations. Conversations about performance. Often brief, but always meaningful. In the best organizations, there is an openness and directness not found in less successful organizations. There is pride, loyalty, trust, and a sense of ownership fostered by an effective recognition strategy that mixes tangible and intangible reinforcement for frequent incremental improvements, not just for recognition of annual accomplishments. They celebrate wins. And they win often!

Some Remedies

☐ **1. Design a formal process for recognizing outstanding performance.**
It's hard to beat the value of spontaneous, informal recognition, but you'll benefit, too, from some structure. A formal recognition process can leverage spontaneous, informal recognition and provide your organization with consistency, ensure broad coverage across the employee population, create metrics that enable you to continuously improve the process, promote equity, and establish financial controls. Start by setting goals for the recognition strategy. Goals that align with organizational objectives.

Then design a process that is easy to administer and easy to explain to employees. Your communication around the process should establish the rationale and intent in simple language. Be especially careful to set expectations around tangible rewards. Establish the link between your recognition efforts and the organization's business strategy. Establish schedules, baseline goals and metrics, and, very importantly, a budget for providing recognition. A good recognition process will not put a limit on the number of employees who can be formally recognized, but it should limit recognition to real accomplishments. Employees need to be clear about that, absolutely clear about what it takes to earn rewards and formal recognition. Make sure to build some flexibility into your programs. Include guidelines for informal recognition. It's critical to ensure that managers understand that a formal recognition program is only the organization-level framework and does not in any way substitute for the primary role managers play in providing personalized, spontaneous, and informal recognition.

☐ **2. Align your recognition process with organizational strategy, values, and all HR practices.** Alignment should occur in several dimensions. First, align to strategy. Consider your organization's high-level strategic objectives and make sure you're recognizing the behaviors and accomplishments that support your strategy. Remember that people don't necessarily do what they're paid to do. People generally pay attention to what gets measured and, in the long run, only put in sustained effort for what gets recognized and reinforced. If your strategic intent is to develop your business by creating deep-seated and intimate customer relationships, don't recognize efficiency at the expense of customer service. Of course, it's not a bad idea to recognize the employee who implements an idea for increasing efficiency. But if the vast majority of recognition is given to cost-cutting rather than customer service, employees will get the message and your customer-focused strategy will likely be doomed. Recognize all good performance but focus formal recognition on the behaviors and accomplishments that drive your strategy. Second, align to culture. Culture reflects what you care about and how things get done in your organization. Do you want a culture that's informal, entrepreneurial, and fast? Or, is the organization better served by a culture that's more formal, methodical, analytical, and thorough? The focus of your recognition will help shape your culture just as it will help drive your strategy. Finally, align employee recognition to all talent management processes. All these practices should be aligned to each other; everything should work together. How is your recognition practice linked to a total rewards strategy that includes compensation and benefits? To performance management? To succession? The point is, you can't implement an employee-recognition initiative, or any other talent management practice for that matter, in isolation and expect it to achieve its potential impact. Those organizations that break out of the pack are the ones that have aligned and integrated all their talent management practices so they reinforce and leverage each other. It's not about individual ingredients—it's the entire stew!

☐ **3. Individualize reinforcement and recognition.** People. Remarkably similar, yet each individual truly unique. How well do you know your people? Do you know what they care about? What motivates them? You should. And if you don't, why not ask them? Ask about their hobbies, interests, and vacations. This information will come in handy when providing individualized, tangible but non-cash recognition. Studies have shown that non-cash reinforcement is up to 50% more cost-effective in motivating people than cash. In other words, Jane Employee will likely find a $250 monogrammed golf bag to be just as rewarding, just as motivating, as $500 in cash. That's assuming, of course, that Jane is a golfer. And that's why it pays to know your employees' interests. Learn how they want to be recognized and personalize your recognition. Some employees will be ecstatic when you offer them a half-day off as a reward for long hours they put in over the past week to meet a critical business objective. Other employees wouldn't respond so positively, might even view it as a punishing consequence of their good performance. Don't inadvertently punish a self-conscious, introverted employee by praising her in public when she'd rather have a discreet, private show of appreciation. Don't deny your self-assured hotshot the public recognition he craves by delivering your praise in private. It's simple. Just know your employees and treat them like they want to be treated. Empower your managers to treat people as individuals. Make sure your policies and procedures are flexible to accommodate as many individuals as possible.

☐ **4. Engage senior management in personally providing recognition.** The most effective employee recognition occurs in organizations that have high levels of senior management participation. The active involvement of high-level leaders provides a model for mid-level managers and sets a tone for the entire organization. Top management adds credibility to recognition and can significantly increase the meaningfulness of recognition for employees. Awards ceremonies and celebrations give senior management an opportunity to reinforce the link between strategy and individual contributions, to emphasize key messages, and to strengthen levels of trust in the organization. Establish ways for high performers to get personally recognized by senior management for a job well done.

An e-mail, phone call, or personal note from someone at the top of the organization is a great way to get recognition.

☐ **5. Learn to celebrate wins.** Winners celebrate. Celebrate often. Major victories. Small improvements. Anything positive is an opportunity for celebration. Celebrations can be formal—like awards banquets—to simple—like unplanned hallway gatherings to recognize the two employees who just tag-teamed to save an important customer account. Learn how to celebrate. Invite the right people. Depending on the situation, it may be appropriate to include employees outside the immediate workgroup, bosses several levels up, customers, even family members. Select the right people to provide the recognition. Again, the situation should dictate who presents the recognition. A peer may be an appropriate presenter and feel honored when asked to provide recognition for others. In addition to the immediate boss who is generally a key presenter, the presence of one or more senior executives can provide great emphasis for special occasions. Incorporate symbolism that supports your engagement and business strategies and fits your culture. Consider how awards, trophies, and language can be used to add meaning to the celebration. Vocabulary is important, and it's often effective to coin terms to identify a team, an initiative, or a process. There's a reason that sports teams have unique names, mascots, trophies, fight songs, and cheerleaders. Keep it all genuine, and monitor the employee pulse to gauge how things are working. If there's a lack of interest or, even worse, an undercurrent of mocking or sarcasm about the celebration, make adjustments. That's a big part of learning how to celebrate. Sincerity and authenticity are essential. Timeliness is important, too. Provide recognition and celebrate as soon as practical after the event being celebrated. And, of course, make sure it's really deserved, that it's about real success. Celebrate successes often and have fun with it!

☐ **6. Use an appropriate mix of tangible and intangible reinforcement.** Tangible can be touched. Cash is top on that list, but far from the only thing. Non-cash tangible reinforcement should be your first consideration for providing "spot bonuses" to recognize extraordinary effort and accomplishment. Rewards can range from simple—a pair of movie tickets—to extravagant—an all-expenses-paid weekend in Manhattan with theatre tickets and fine dining. Make the most of your rewards budget by using non-cash tangible rewards. Movie tickets costing $16 will be remembered by the employee far longer than a $20 bill. Such thoughtfulness builds employee loyalty. Never underestimate the impact of tangible reinforcement, but never, ever neglect the power of intangible reinforcement. Intangible reinforcement is the manager's best tool for motivating employees on a day-to-day basis because it's free and it's effective. Research reveals that spontaneous recognition from the immediate boss is at or near the top of the list of preferred rewards by most employees. Pats on the back, words of praise, and handwritten notes—all have incredible meaning to employees. Exposure to senior executives is also valuable. Copy managers up the line on e-mails and voice mails to increase the impact of recognition. Whatever the method, make sure the recognition is genuine—that the manager believes the message. That it's legitimate—actually follows good performance. And that it's meaningful—delivered in a context and format that the employee values.

☐ **7. Educate management on how and when to provide reinforcement.** How much? How often? Can there be too much of a good thing? Can you overdo recognition? Can there be too much reinforcement for stellar performance? Sure, it's possible. Not likely, but possible. Get the proportion right. Positive reinforcement should occur every day for every employee. It's not true reinforcement unless it follows something done well, and that means reinforcement and recognition isn't limited to major accomplishments. Incremental improvements in behavior should be reinforced, too. When new skills and behaviors are being learned, reinforcement and recognition should be very frequent. Once good performance is established, it's more effective to provide it intermittently. In every case, reinforcement is most effective when it's provided immediately and clearly specifies the behavior or accomplishment being recognized. Provide a level of recognition and reward that's appropriate for the degree of accomplishment.

☐ **8. Develop feedback, coaching, and conflict-management skills in the management ranks.** Are your managers and executives well prepared to provide effective recognition and reinforcement? If they are, your organization is the anomaly. Year after year the research conducted on 360° survey data has been consistent and clearly identifies the skills in which managers and executives excel and in which they fall short. Out of 67 competencies in the Lominger Leadership Architect® Competency Library, the ones at the bottom, the skills with which managers consistently struggle, are related to dealing with people. Consider this list of the 12 lowest-ranked competencies: Developing Direct Reports and Others (67th), Personal Learning, Understanding Others, Confronting Direct Reports, Managing Vision and Purpose, Conflict Management, Dealing with Paradox, Managing Through Systems, Motivating Others, Directing Others, Personal Disclosure, and Patience. If you throw Listening, Sizing Up People, and Presentation Skills into the list, you've pretty well defined the competencies managers need to effectively engage in meaningful conversations about performance, to effectively coach, to effectively reinforce and recognize. So, what are you doing to develop these skills in your organization? Begin by setting expectations that these are important skills for leaders. Training can be a launching pad for developing these skills, and training methods for interpersonal skills should use lots of role-play and action learning. But it's primarily on the job that these competencies are developed. Assess them on the job and provide feedback and coaching to develop them.

☐ **9. Create a high-performance culture that recognizes and differentially rewards top performance.** Culture critically impacts organizational performance because it guides how we do our work and how we think about our work. It's a reflection of our collective attitudes, beliefs, and values. Culture shapes how decisions are made, how fast the organization moves, how it takes risks, and how it develops talent. Culture affects employee engagement, recruitment, and retention. It directly affects the organization's performance. Organizations that create high-performance cultures empower their managers to provide meaningful consequences and help them understand how to do that. In those organizations, management is largely about managing consequences because only positive and certain consequences sustain performance over the long haul. Those high-performance cultures don't tolerate minimum performance. The focus is all about optimum performance, about becoming faster, better, leaner, more profitable every day, every quarter, every year. The business strategy is clearly communicated and rewards and recognition are structured to reinforce that strategy. Strategy is translated into goals and measures. Everyone knows what to do, how to do it, and what to expect in return. Simply put, talented people work best when they have a set of goals and measures and differentiated rewards for success. Differentiation is the key. In the best organizations there is an openness and directness not found in less successful organizations. There is pride, loyalty, trust, and a sense of ownership fostered by the effective reward and recognition strategy that blends tangible and intangible reinforcement as a consequence for frequent incremental improvements, not just for recognition of annual accomplishments.

☐ **10. Implement a best-in-class performance management process.** Get your performance management process right. We know that a well-designed and administered performance management process drives organizational performance for several reasons. Performance management aligns employee efforts with the strategic intent of the organization. It differentiates between levels of performance and helps create a high-performance culture. And, the research is crystal clear—people perform better when they have specific goals and when they receive feedback on their performance. Did you also know that your performance management process can be one of the primary vehicles through which you deliver both formal and informal employee recognition? In fact, recognition will occur as a matter of course when the process is working as it should because meaningful conversations are the centerpiece of all good performance management systems. Meaningful conversations are perceived by employees as recognition. It tells employees that management pays attention to their work, that management cares enough to listen and to coach and to provide honest and direct feedback. Of course, this won't occur if there is no managerial courage. Saying what needs to be said at the right time, to the right person, in the right manner. Managerial courage is speaking up and being willing to take some heat. Too often organizations prepare managers to engage in performance management by teaching them the mechanics of the process—how to use a software program or how to properly fill out a paper instrument. They teach them about schedules, and what must be turned in to HR before merit pay increases can be administered. All of that administrative stuff will do little or nothing to improve performance, to drive meaningful conversations, to provide recognition. This is frequently a fatal flaw in how performance management is implemented. The real issue is managerial courage that drives meaningful conversations. This is what performance management is really all about. This is where your focus should be—in facilitating those discussions. Give your managers the tools and language and skills to provide feedback and coaching. Help them to develop managerial courage so they embrace transparency, so they truly differentiate performance, so they have honest and frank conversations about performance. Model this behavior. Make meaningful conversations a cornerstone of your culture.

Everyone has an invisible sign hanging from their neck saying,
'Make me feel important.'
Mary Kay Ash – Founder, Mary Kay Cosmetics

Suggested Readings

Bielaszka-DuVernay, C. (2007). Are you using recognition effectively? *Harvard Management Update, 12*(5), 2-3.

Connellan, T. K. (2003). *Bringing out the best in others! Three keys for business leaders, educators, coaches and parents.* Austin, TX: Bard Press.

Dai, G., & De Meuse, K. P. (2007). *The 2006 International VOICES® norms: North America, Europe, Asia, and New Zealand/Australia.* Minneapolis, MN: Lominger International: A Korn/Ferry Company.

Daniels, A. C. (2000). *Bringing out the best in people: How to apply the astonishing power of positive reinforcement.* NY: McGraw-Hill.

Davidson, L. (1999). The power of personal recognition. *Workforce, 78*(7), 44-48.

Eichinger, R. W., Ruyle, K. E., & Lombardo, M. M. (2007). *FYI for performance management™.* Minneapolis, MN: Lominger International: A Korn/Ferry Company.

Fournies, F. F. (1999). *Coaching for improved work performance.* NY: McGraw-Hill.

Gostick, A., & Elton, C. (2001). *Managing with carrots: Using recognition to attract and retain the best people.* Layton, UT: Gibbs Smith.

Hale, R. L., & Maehling, R. F. (1992). *Recognition redefined: Building self-esteem at work.* Minneapolis, MN: Tennant Company.

Kouzes, J. M., & Posner, B. Z. (2002). *The leadership challenge.* San Francisco: John Wiley & Sons.

Kouzes, J. M., & Posner, B. Z. (2003). *Encouraging the heart: A leader's guide to rewarding and recognizing others.* San Francisco: Jossey-Bass.

Lawler, E. E., III., & Lawler, E. E. (2003). *Treat people right: How organizations and employees can create a win/win relationship to achieve high performance at all levels.* San Francisco: Jossey-Bass.

Ludwick, P. (2006). Just say "Thank you. I appreciate it." *Public Management, 88*(2), 31-32.

Luthans, F., & Stajkovic, A. D. (1999). Reinforce for performance: The need to go beyond pay and even rewards. *Academy of Management Executive, 13*, 49-57.

Nelson, B. (2005). *1001 Ways to reward employees.* NY: Workman.

Rampersad, H. K. (2003). *Total performance scorecard: Redefining management to achieve performance with integrity.* Boston, MA: Butterworth-Heinemann.

Robbins, M., & Carlson, R. (2007). *Focus on the good stuff: The power of appreciation.* San Francisco: John Wiley & Sons.

Saunderson, R. (2004). Survey findings of the effectiveness of employee recognition in the public sector. *Public Personnel Management, 33*, 255-274.

Sirota, D., Mischkind, L. A., & Meltzer, M. I. (2005). *The enthusiastic employee: How companies profit by giving workers what they want.* Upper Saddle River, NJ: Pearson Education.

Stajkovic, A. D., & Luthans, F. (1997). A meta-analysis of the effects of organization behavior modification on task performance, 1975–1995. *Academy of Management Journal, 40*, 1122-1149.

Swindell, C. (2007). *Engaged leadership: Building a culture to overcome employee disengagement.* Hoboken, NJ: John Wiley & Sons.

Ulrich, D., Zenger, J., & Smallwood, N. (1999). *Results-based leadership.* Boston, MA: Harvard Business School Press.

Wiley, C. (1997). What motivates employees according to over 40 years of motivation surveys. *International Journal of Manpower, 18*, 263-280.

Engagement Driver K
Pay Fairness

One man's wage increase is another man's price increase.
Harold Wilson – British politician and Prime Minister

The Signpost

Think money's not important? That it doesn't motivate? Think again. Research studies have repeatedly shown a link between financial incentives and job performance and levels of motivation. Money can motivate, but it can also demotivate when employees sense a lack of internal pay equity, when the compensation of coworkers is not commensurate with their contribution. It happens, too, when employees don't see external pay equity, when they're not being compensated as well as they would be for doing the same job in another firm. Executing a well-thought-out compensation strategy is essential to motivating, engaging, and retaining employees.

Unskilled

- ☐ Unwilling or unable to discriminate between high and low performers
- ☐ Misses the mark on internal equity; plays favorites
- ☐ Bases compensation decisions only on market data
- ☐ Uses inappropriate mix of base pay and variable compensation
- ☐ Rewards management even when overall business performance misses targets
- ☐ Does not align recognition initiatives with business goals and organizational culture
- ☐ Fails to understand workforce motivators; relies solely on tangible rewards to motivate
- ☐ Avoids candid conversations with employees about their performance
- ☐ Maintains shroud of secrecy around compensation strategy
- ☐ Centralizes all compensation decisions; excludes line management
- ☐ Ineffectively measures employee behavior and accomplishments
- ☐ Fails to clearly set expectations and communicate goals

Skilled

- ☐ Aligns compensation strategy with business strategy and all human capital practices
- ☐ Accurately analyzes jobs and compensable factors

☐ Effectively uses a combination of variable compensation and long-term incentives

☐ Clearly communicates the total rewards strategy to all employees

☐ Exercises courage to discriminate and differentiate; rewards high performers at the expense of low performers

☐ Engages and empowers line managers to make compensation decisions

☐ Makes job bands, related salary ranges, and career paths transparent

☐ Clearly communicates expectations and performance goals

☐ Clearly defines the link between performance and rewards

☐ Establishes effective measures of behavior and of accomplishments

☐ Keeps up with compensation trends and changes in marketplace conditions

☐ Follows through with bonus commitments; pays when targets are met and does not pay when they are missed

Some Causes

☐ Lack of business acumen

☐ Conflict avoidance

☐ Unwillingness to consider new approaches to compensation

☐ Lack of listening and understanding what motivates workforce

☐ Failure to discriminate performance levels and treat people differently

☐ Poor internal communication

☐ Unsophisticated talent management practices

☐ Us vs. them (management vs. employees) mentality

☐ Tolerance for mediocrity

☐ Low levels of trust

The Ten Leadership Architect® Competencies Most Associated with This Engagement Driver *(in order of connectedness)*

13. Confronting Direct Reports
23. Fairness to Direct Reports
35. Managing and Measuring Work
56. Sizing Up People
36. Motivating Others
5. Business Acumen
12. Conflict Management
52. Process Management
20. Directing Others
46. Perspective

The Map

Researchers have consistently debunked Frederick Herzberg's claim that extrinsic rewards don't motivate. Studies have repeatedly shown a correlation between financial incentives and job performance and, additionally, that those tangible rewards positively impact intrinsic motivation. But if money is distributed inequitably, it demotivates. So, it's important to address internal and external pay equity, but forward-thinking organizations go beyond equity. They employ innovative compensation strategies that propel individuals and the business forward to achieve key performance objectives. In recent years, there has been a large increase in the number of organizations that pay for knowledge and mastery of critical competencies. There has also been a significant increase in the use of flexible benefits as part of a total rewards strategy. Creative use of incentives is also on the rise, including incentives that reward teams. An increase in the proportion of variable pay awarded to employees at all levels has been accompanied by a decline in seniority pay. Such practices based on years of company service are rapidly disappearing from the compensation arena. The organizations that best manage compensation do so by considering the big picture of human capital. They align all their people strategies so they work together and strengthen the desired culture and drive organizational performance. As an example of this, consider two organizations. One selects a compensation strategy that pays above-market rates in an attempt to better attract and retain talent and achieve higher levels of organizational performance. But, they do so without attending to other human capital practices that reinforce their strategic intent. They don't implement a rigorous performance management system. They don't prepare their line managers to have meaningful performance conversations. And they fail to clearly communicate performance expectations. The result: financial performance of the firm suffers because payroll expenses increase without moving the needle on organizational performance. Another organization selects the same compensation strategy—above-market pay rates—but also implements other human capital practices that lead to a high-performance culture. The result: financial performance of the firm soars, they attract and retain the best talent, and engagement levels rise significantly. Your compensation strategy is a primary lever for driving organizational performance. Do whatever it takes to get it right.

Some Remedies

☐ **1. Create a strategic compensation plan aligned with your business strategy, values, and culture.** Simplistic thinking about compensation is a sure route to mediocrity. Do you only consider market rates? Do you allow the market to control your compensation structures? Or do you model your compensation after the competition? On the surface, these approaches might make sense. But does your competition have an identical strategy? An identical culture? Identical talent? Most assuredly not. It follows, then, that modeling your compensation strategy on the competition or the broader labor market will result in mediocrity at best. Rather than letting the tail wag the dog, take control. Step back. Look at the big picture. Be strategic. What is your business? Where are you taking the business? What kind of talent do you need to get there? Your compensation strategy— your total rewards strategy—has to be aligned with your business strategy and all your other human capital practices. This is Business 101. What culture are you creating? What outcomes do you want? What's required of employees to achieve those outcomes? How will you measure it? You've got to answer these questions to guide compensation decisions. Create a total rewards strategy that will drive your business in the direction you desire. When you align rewards with business goals, you'll establish a partnership with the workforce in which everyone wins—employees, management, shareholders, and customers. You have many rewards tools at your disposal: base pay, a myriad of variable compensation methods, and a vast array of non-cash benefits. Pick and choose the tools that will accomplish your strategic objectives. Use base pay to reward ongoing individual contribution. Base pay should match an individual's sustained performance, the knowledge and skill they bring to the table and, of course, should meet or exceed their worth in the labor market. Use variable pay to reward achievements, the results delivered by the individual or team. In addition to variable compensation in the form of cash, be sure to consider ownership in the enterprise and/or profit sharing as a reward for results. There are many ways to do this, including grants, options, gainsharing, and various forms of profit sharing. Non-cash benefits are also part of the total rewards strategy and can play a very important role in attracting and retaining talent and shaping the culture of your organization. The variety of available benefit options is immense. Each is a tool that can accelerate or retard the achievement of your strategic objectives. Remember, you're in control. So pick the rewards tools that support your strategic intent, that strengthen your culture, and that align with and leverage your other human capital practices.

☐ **2. Implement a communication plan that provides a line of sight between business strategy and compensation.** And not just your business strategy. Share your compensation strategy, too. Let employees have a line of sight that allows them to connect the business strategy to compensation decisions. What are the key roles in your organization, the roles in which you're investing more heavily for strategic reasons? Employees should know. How do you analyze jobs? What are the compensable factors you reward? Employees should know. Your strategy around variable compensation deserves special focus. Spell it out clearly for employees so they understand without question what's expected, what's rewarded, to what extent, and when. Communicate early and often. Provide regular updates, preferably on a monthly basis, so that employees know where they currently stand in terms of bonuses and other variable compensation. Don't surprise them! Even when the news is bad, give it to them straight. Matter-of-factly report results the same way every month. Some months will look good. Others won't. Don't make a big deal one way or the other. You want to engage the workforce, right? Then take the covers off and provide some transparency. Give them the formulas used for bonus calculation. Allow them to run scenarios. Really engage them in understanding and actively contributing to the business.

☐ **3. Accurately assess jobs, especially key jobs, to clearly understand and address compensable factors.** Employee engagement increases when employees are in jobs that provide them with meaningful intrinsic rewards and equitable extrinsic rewards. Naturally, you'll consider the needs of the business when designing jobs. That's great. But don't neglect the needs of the workforce. When a well-designed job is staffed with the right person, the employee will have a highly favorable view of these factors:

- *Information:* There is clear communication about expectations and feedback on performance.
- *Task Variety:* The job provides an opportunity to use a variety of skills.
- *Importance:* The job delivers something important to others.
- *Freedom:* There is an appropriate level of independence afforded in doing the job.

Even if you've attended to these factors when designing a job, you'll still have a disengaged employee if you do a poor job of selection when hiring. What constitutes meaningful information, task variety, job importance, and freedom differs from one person to another. You can err in either direction—by setting the selection bar too low or too high. Too low and you've got major problems on your hands—employees who, even if motivated, deliver poor performance and lack the capability of ever developing the skills the job requires. Too high and you'll soon have engagement issues because the intrinsic motivation isn't there. You've got great talent on the bus, but the ride is never going to please the overqualified employee unless you change the job to fit the employee. So job design is important, and it impacts compensation because the design of the job will dictate the compensable factors—the skill required to do the work, the level of responsibility, the amount of effort required, and the conditions in which the work is performed. Put lots of thought into job design so the right work gets done the right way by the right employees. When you do, you'll get better quality, better productivity, and a more engaged workforce.

☐ **4. Employ a pay-for-performance strategy that addresses both individual and team contributions.** When you pay for performance, you're not paying jobs. You're paying individuals and teams. Job design is important for the reasons described above. The job design and your compensation strategy will determine the position level, will place the job in a particular pay band, and will put some definition to the upper and lower bounds of compensation for the job. But if you pay jobs instead of paying for individual and team contribution, you won't necessarily be rewarding performance, and you'll lose out on an opportunity to drive your organization forward. Research clearly shows that organizations that consistently reward individuals *and* teams for performance outperform those that don't. To successfully pay for performance, address the following:

- *Communication:* Carefully communicate goals and metrics and define how achievement will impact variable compensation. Ensure that everyone in the organization understands and accepts the plan that is laid out prior to the start of the business cycle.

- *Differentiation:* Deliver rewards that match the contribution of individuals. Top contributors should get the lion's share of the rewards.

- *Managerial Courage:* Pay-for-performance won't work if your managers are unwilling to objectively assess performance, make the hard calls, and have the tough conversations.

- *Internal Competition:* Business is a team sport. Consider how to reward teams or organizational units in addition to, or even in lieu of, individual rewards. The key is to make sure that you're not setting up a situation in which an individual or team can win by making another individual or team within the organization lose.

Research suggests a well-designed pay-for-performance system will return up to four times the cost of variable compensation. Not only that, but implementing a pay-for-performance practice will increase the likelihood of attracting, engaging, and retaining the very best talent. Design it carefully. Communicate it clearly. Train for it thoroughly. And reinforce it continually.

☐ **5. Set performance targets carefully so they can be achieved but only with significant effort.** Most businesses define success with high-level aggregated measures. Operating income. Return on assets. Revenue growth. Earnings per share. Market share. Customer loyalty. All important stuff. But the key is to translate goals for all that important stuff into meaningful measures for employees at all levels. As you set goals and targets for your pay-for-performance practice, make sure you've answered the following questions:

- *Are the goals aligned with the business strategies?* The most effective goals start at the top of the organization and cascade down through business units, departments, and teams to each individual. At each level, the goals increase in specificity so they can be embraced and owned by that particular level. The result is an array of tailored performance goals reflecting the firm's strategic intent that are distributed throughout the organization and owned by each group and each individual.

- *Are goals appropriate for the level?* Performance goals should describe achievements that are within the control of the performer. To the extent possible, the performer should be able to directly affect the variables that impact the outcome. This will typically vary with the position level of the performer. The higher one goes in an organization, the more accomplishments depend on the work of others and are subject to the unexpected things that happen in the real world. Goals should reflect that reality. The best goals are shaped to fit the role and, as much as possible, rely on individual performance, not on external factors.

- *Can they be measured?* Put a number to your performance goals. Make them quantifiable. People pay attention to what gets measured. If you can't measure it, you can't evaluate it or manage it. Choose metrics for which measurement methods and processes exist, for which the cost of measurement is not prohibitive, and for which there is shared understanding of the meaning.

- *Have you put in the right amount of stretch?* Build in stretch to extend the employee's reach and impact. Generally, people perform best with achievable stretch goals—goals that can realistically be reached by standing tall and putting forth significant effort. Goals set too high or too low demotivate. Goals that are too high are seen as unreasonable and result in employees making token, half-hearted efforts. Goals that are too low let people coast and encourage them to lose focus. This is a balancing act complicated by the need to set stretch goals for individuals as well as business units. Set the bar high, but not completely out of reach.

- *Do you have funding?* Financially based metrics are generally self-funding. You need to have a budget for non-financial metrics that don't directly result in increased income or cash flow.

- *Have you defined the appropriate performance period?* You can have different performance periods and payout intervals for different levels of employees. You can expect that higher position levels have responsibility for metrics that span a longer time horizon, and individuals at higher levels should have increased tolerance for delayed gratification. They might have some incentives paid out annually and other long-term incentives paid out even less frequently. However, first-line employees may benefit from quarterly payouts.

- *Have you considered the interaction of metrics?* Usually it takes a combination of metrics, often interdependent, to achieve desired results. If you only reward quality, productivity is likely to suffer. If you only reward efficiency, customer service might take a hit. So consider when it's appropriate to identify a combination of goals that must all be achieved in order to get the rewards.

- *At what level are incentives paid out?* Consider using at least some level of individual incentives when individual accomplishment can be readily measured, when results are mostly in control of the individual, and when there is little probability of creating destructive internal competition. Team incentives encourage collaboration but work best when there is at least some differential applied to recognize individual contribution within the team. The trifecta is an incentive system that uses a combination of individual, team, and company-wide incentives. The trick is to design it so it's straightforward and simple enough for employees to understand and manageable to administer.

☐ **6. Be consistent and follow through as planned when paying out incentives; don't change rules midstream.** Stand firm. Pay-for-performance systems are sure to fail when organizations change rules in the middle of the game. It's just as important to not pay out incentives when goals are missed as it is to pay when goals are met. Failure on either count demonstrates a lack of managerial accountability and destroys trust. Be consistent. Set realistic stretch targets and then don't backpedal when it becomes obvious that goals will be missed. Consistency and follow-through are important in how incentives are paid out. If you preach performance and set expectations that top performers are going to get the bulk of the rewards, better make sure they really do. It's all about managerial courage and integrity. Pay-for-performance doesn't work in the absence of courage. It doesn't work in the absence of integrity.

☐ **7. Increase the transparency of job bands, related salary ranges, and career paths.** Become an open book. Compensation is a sensitive subject, and making compensation public is considered taboo in most work cultures. Ironically, there is research evidence that secrecy creates more troubles than does openness. In a vacuum, employees can make all kinds of assumptions that lead to perceived inequities. Better that the pay scales—at least the ranges for pay grades—are clearly communicated and there is no secret about employee grades. This becomes even more important at higher pay grades. Threatened? Why? At least give this issue some serious thought. Openness will foster trust, not suspicion. While you're at it, consider how you can provide more information to employees about the organization's performance. Opening your financial books to the extent possible engenders a sense of ownership, loyalty, trust, and helps employees see ways they contribute to the organization's success. Openness is a hallmark of high-performance cultures.

☐ **8. Empower line managers to make compensation decisions within specified budget constraints.** It's a huge mistake to take compensation decisions out of the hands of line managers. They are the ones closest to the performance of their employees. They are in the best position to assess performance. To have performance discussions. To really impact performance. Management is largely about managing consequences. If you prevent your line managers from making compensation decisions, you've made their jobs immeasurably more difficult. Of course, managers need to have guidelines and clear policies to follow. They need to have budgets for variable compensation. And they need to be responsible, accountable for their decisions. When they have that accountability, they are more likely to follow through on all their responsibilities—communicating the business strategy, explaining the compensation strategy, clearly setting expectations, providing feedback and coaching, and dealing with problem performers early.

☐ **9. Educate line managers on compensation practices and provide tools to facilitate compensation decisions.** Talk is cheap. Execution is difficult. Execution is in the hands of line managers who typically cringe at the thought of making pay decisions. That's understandable. Compensation is a complex subject. It's hard work to differentiate performance objectively and accurately. And it's uncomfortable to tell employees they aren't receiving merit pay because their performance didn't stack up. Give your line management tools to simplify the process. Educate them on your compensation strategy and philosophy. Give them lots of practice in having performance-related conversations and assessing performance. Reinforce and reward the managers who do it best. If you fail here, you'll have managers taking the easy route, applying variable compensation across their employees like sunblock—a little dab for everyone. Or, they'll pass the buck and claim variable compensation decisions are out of their hands. The rubber meets the road in the conversations between line managers and their employees. Make sure they've got the skills and confidence to do their jobs.

☐ **10. Engage resources so the firm keeps up with compensation trends and changes in marketplace conditions.** Compensation is complex and requires specialized expertise. Think twice before going it alone. A compensation specialist can prevent costly missteps. Also, consider joining one or more of the professional organizations that provide resources:

- WorldatWork: The Total Rewards Association
  http://www.worldatwork.org/waw/home/html/home.jsp
- Society for Human Resource Management
  http://www.shrm.org/
- International Foundation of Employee Benefit Plans
  http://www.ifebp.org/
- International Association for Human Resource Information Management
  http://www.ihrim.org/
- Employee Benefit Research Institute
  http://www.ebri.org/
- American Benefits Council
  http://www.americanbenefitscouncil.org/

I don't pay good wages because I have a lot of money;
I have a lot of money because I pay good wages.
Robert Bosch – German industrialist and founder, Robert Bosch GmbH

Suggested Readings

Cawood, S., & Bailey, R. V. (2006). *Destination profit: Creating people-profit opportunities in your organization*. Mountain View, CA: Davies-Black.

Chingos, P. T. (2002). *Paying for performance: A guide to compensation management* (2nd ed.). NY: John Wiley & Sons.

Eisenberger, R., & Armeli, S. (1997). Can salient reward increase creative performance without reducing intrinsic creative interest? *Journal of Personality and Social Psychology, 72*, 652-663.

Eisenberger, R., Rhoades, L., & Cameron, J. (1999). Does pay for performance increase or decrease perceived self-determination and intrinsic motivation? *Journal of Personality and Social Psychology, 77*, 1026-1040.

Gerhart, B., & Rynes, S. L. (2003). *Compensation: Theory, evidence, and strategic implications*. Thousand Oaks, CA: Sage.

Gilliland, S. W., & Langdon, J. C. (1998). Creating performance management systems that promote perception of fairness. In J. W. Smither (Ed.), *Performance appraisal: State of the art in practice*. San Francisco: Jossey-Bass.

Greenberg, J., & McCarty, C. L. (1990). The interpersonal aspects of procedural justice: A new perspective on pay fairness. *Labor Law Journal, 41*, 580-586.

Heneman, R. L. (2001). *Corporate business strategies and compensation strategies*. NY: AMACOM.

Heneman, R. L., Fisher, M. M., & Dixon, K. E. (2001). Reward and organizational systems alignment. *Compensation & Benefits Review, 33*(6), 18-30.

Heneman, R. L., Ledford, G. E., & Gresham, M. T. (2000). The changing nature of work and its effects on compensation design and delivery. In R. L. Heneman (Ed.), *Strategic reward management: Design, implementation, and evaluation*. Greenwich, CT: Information Age Publishing.

Kerr, S. (1975). On the folly of rewarding A, while hoping for B. *Academy of Management Journal, 18*(4), 769-783.

Kouzes, J. M., & Posner, B. Z. (2002). *The leadership challenge*. San Francisco: John Wiley & Sons.

Lawler, E. E. (1981). Merit pay: Fact or fiction? *Management Review, 70*(4), 50-54.

Lawler, E. E., III. (2003). *Treat people right: How organizations and employees can create a win/win relationship to achieve high performance at all levels*. San Francisco: Jossey-Bass.

Lawler, E. E., III., & Worley, C. G. (2006). Winning support for organizational change: Designing employee reward systems that keep on working. *Ivey Business Journal, 70*(4), 1-5.

Luthans, F., & Stajkovic, A. D. (1999). Reinforce for performance: The need to go beyond pay and even rewards. *Academy of Management Executive, 13*, 49-57.

Martocchio, J. J. (2004). *Strategic compensation: A human resource management approach* (3rd ed.). Upper Saddle River, NJ: Pearson Education.

K

McShane, S. L., & Von Glinow, M. A. (2008). *Organizational behavior: Emerging realities for the workplace revolution* (4th ed.). NY: McGraw-Hill/Irwin.

Ramaswami, S. N., & Singh, J. (2003). Antecedents and consequences of merit pay fairness for industrial salespeople. *Journal of Marketing, 67*, 46-66.

Rampersad, H. K. (2003). *Total performance scorecard: Redefining management to achieve performance with integrity*. Boston, MA: Butterworth-Heinemann.

Shore, T. H., Tashchian, A., & Jourdan, L. (2006). Effects of internal and external pay comparisons on work attitudes. *Journal of Applied Social Psychology, 10*, 2578-2598.

Sirota, D., Mischkind, L. A., & Meltzer, M. I. (2005). *The enthusiastic employee: How companies profit by giving workers what they want*. Upper Saddle River, NJ: Pearson Education.

Stack, J., & Burlingham, B. (1994). *The great game of business*. NY: Doubleday Currency.

Stajkovic, A. D., & Luthans, F. (1997). A meta-analysis of the effects of organization behavior modification on task performance, 1975-1995. *Academy of Management Journal, 40*, 1122-1149.

Towers Perrin. (2003). *The 2003 Towers Perrin Talent Report: Working today: Understanding what drives employee engagement*. Retrieved January 15, 2009, from http://www.towersperrin.com/tp/getwebcachedoc?webc=HRS/USA/2003/200309/Talent_2003.pdf

Ulrich, D., Eichinger, R. W., Kulas, J. T., & De Meuse, K. P. (2007). *50 More things you need to know: The science behind best people practices for managers & HR professionals*. Minneapolis, MN: Lominger International: A Korn/Ferry Company.

Ulrich, D., Zenger, J., & Smallwood, N. (1999). *Results-based leadership*. Boston, MA: Harvard Business School Press.

Wiley, C. (1997). What motivates employees according to over 40 years of motivation surveys. *International Journal of Manpower, 18*, 263-280.

Zingheim, P. K., & Schuster, J. R. (2000). *Pay people right: Breakthrough reward strategies to create great companies*. San Francisco: Jossey-Bass.

K